THE AVENGING FURY OF THE PLAINS

JOHN "LIVER-EATING" JOHNSTON

EXPLODING THE MYTHS – DISCOVERING THE MAN

By Dennis J. McLelland Ed.D

Copyright © 2008 by Dennis J. McLelland

ISBN 0-7414-4527-1

Published by:

INFINITY
PUBLISHING.COM

1094 New DeHaven Street, Suite 100
West Conshohocken, PA 19428-2713
Info@buybooksontheweb.com
www.buybooksontheweb.com
Toll-free (877) BUY BOOK
Local Phone (610) 941-9999
Fax (610) 941-9959

Printed in the United States of America

Printed on Recycled Paper

Published December 2008

Above is one of the last pictures of "Liver-Eating" Johnson, whose experiences with the Sioux Indians are reviewed in an early Gazette reprint of an article that first appeared in a St. Louis newspaper 46 years ago. The story gives another version of the incident by which Johnson acquired his nickname. As the article appeared only 13 years after Johnson is reported to have eaten the liver of a Sioux Indian, this version may have greater claim to accuracy than others that came later.

Picture 2
Liver-Eating Johnston in 1899.

Notice that Johnston's problems were with the **_Sioux_** – not the **_Crow_**. Johnston's picture was reprinted in the 1912 Billings Gazette. Johnston was near death in this picture.

Acknowledgments

First, and foremost, I want to express how important the late Mr. Harry Owens of Red Lodge, Montana, was to me in encouraging me to write my book. Harry was a life-long resident of Red Lodge and was familiar with the truth about Johnston. Harry disclosed a "secret," in that Johnston's real name was John Garrison. Thanks to my wife, Rosie, for her patience; I also want to thank my brother, Gary McLelland for his assistance and encouragement. Finally, I wish to thank God Almighty for his constant reminders that I'm still a work in progress.

THE GOAL OF THIS BOOK

This book strives to present a true look into the life of John "Liver-Eating" Johnston, undoubtedly one of the most enigmatic historical figures of the old West. It was the goal of this author to offer the reader a twenty-first century evaluation of a highly competent nineteenth-century mountain man. The character, personality, deeds and misdeeds, of John "Garrison" Johnston are clearly presented to the reader. Research has displayed the certainty of one thing- the frontier persona of Liver-Eating Johnston was *invented*. The time has arrived for Johnston to be *re-invented*, in truth, by dismissing myth and embracing reality. It is hoped that the reader will gain an appreciation for the fascinating life of...

John Liver-Eating Johnston

FRIENDS, ACQUAINTENCES & ENEMIES:
"SOMETIMES IT'S HARD TO TELL THE DIFFERENCE"

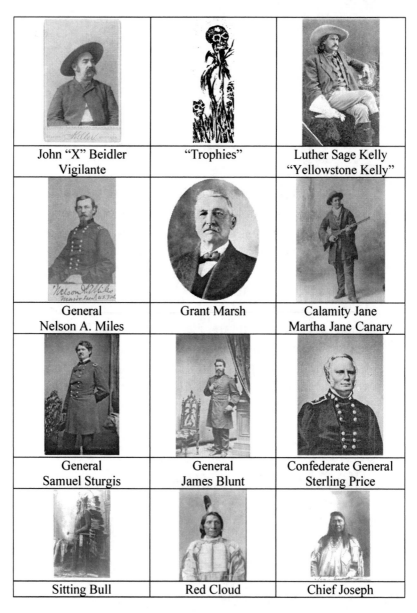

John "X" Beidler Vigilante	"Trophies"	Luther Sage Kelly "Yellowstone Kelly"
General Nelson A. Miles	Grant Marsh	Calamity Jane Martha Jane Canary
General Samuel Sturgis	General James Blunt	Confederate General Sterling Price
Sitting Bull	Red Cloud	Chief Joseph

Picture 3
Who Is Friend? Who Is Foe?

CONTENTS

LIST OF PHOTOGRAPHS

Chronological Timeline of Johnston's Known Activities

July 1824 .... Born near Little York, New Jersey

1838 – 1846 (approx) .... Serves on Whaling Ship/Schooner

1846 – 1848 .... Serves as sailor during Mexican War

1848 – 1858 (approx) .... Remains in Navy or on a Merchant Ship

1858 – 1861 .... Roams the West/Northwest

1862 – 1864 .... Enters Montana - Miner, Trapper, Indian Fighter, Teamster (Wagon Master)

February 1864 – Sept. 1865 .... Scout, Union Army during Civil War

1865 – 1867 .... Teamster – Diamond R Freight Co.

1867 – 1868 .... Woodhawk (wood cutter) with partner "Sims"; earns infamous name of "Liver Eater" at Fort Hawley, Montana Territory, during Sioux battle.

1868 – 1871 .... Woodhawk with pal "X" Beidler".

1869 – 1872 .... Whiskey Peddler at Fort Hamilton, Lethbridge, Alberta Canada

1872 – 1874 .... Whiskey Peddler at Fort Spitzee, Lethbridge, Alberta, Canada

Picture 4
John Johnston during his early sixties (1885/1886)

INTRODUCTION

John "Liver-Eating" Johnston (correct spelling) never ate *anyone's* liver. Then why the name <u>*Liver Eating*</u>? Here is the true story. Johnston earned his macabre name during a battle with the Sioux in 1868. Some researchers think the year of the battle was in 1869, or even 1870. None of that matters because Johnston himself stated that the attack took place in 1868.

The Sioux attacked Johnston and about 15 other wood-cutters as the men were cautiously cutting cords of wood on Sioux land to fuel passing steamboats. Toward the end of the battle, Johnston thrust his knife into a Sioux warrior's side. When he withdrew his knife, a bit of liver remained attached to the knife.

As a joke, Johnston then held up the piece of liver to his friends and asked them if they wanted a taste. Johnston pretended to eat the piece of liver. Hence, the birth of the nickname, "Liver-Eating" Johnston.

The reader is most likely aware that John "Liver-Eating" Johnston was the subject of the 1970's hit movie, *Jeremiah Johnson*, starring Robert Redford. Many viewers of the movie were captivated by the exploits of the movie's protagonist, Jeremiah Johnson, and believed him to be a true historical character. He wasn't. Authors Robert Thorpe and Robert Bunker in a captivating book of historical fiction entitled Crow Killer invented him: *The Saga of Liver Eating Johnson.*

The Avenging Fury of the Plains seeks to assist readers in discovering who the real John Johnston was. Below are the specific research areas from which relevant facts about the life of John "Liver-Eating" Johnston were extracted.

Sources of Research Materials

All sources used to uncover information about Johnston were culled from principally four sources:

1. Government, military, and pension records.
2. Anecdotal recollections of Johnston as recorded by military officers under whom Johnston served as scout during the Indian Wars of 1876-1877.
3. Remembrances of Johnston by acquaintances and friends.
4. Personal interviews with newspaper reporters.

It is indeed difficult to flesh out a full, comprehensive, biography about Liver-Eating Johnston. There are too many "holes" in his personal history. Thus, this book will offer the reader a chronological rendering of many of the known, significant, "life events," that will give readers a solid picture of who John Johnston *truly was* in the early west.

"Wild Bill Hickok" Author Shared Similar Challenge

Joseph G. Rosa, author of "Wild Bill Hickok: The Man & His Myth" (University Press of Kansas, 1996) related a similar dilemma when he wrote, "that in many instances I did unearth new materials, confound legends, and clarify events...that had been a mystery. But there are still gaps, many of them unlikely ever to be filled, for no one can hope to learn everything about another person, least of all a highly controversial historical character."

Johnston Played a Role in Helping to "Open the West."

Johnston did play a role (albeit, a minor one) in the opening of the American west. He served as a scout with the 2nd Colorado Cavalry Volunteers for the Union Army. During the great Indian Wars of 1876-1877, Johnston similarly served as a contract scout for General Nelson A. Miles, General Samuel Sturgis, and many other top-level officers.

"The Avenging Fury of the Plains, John 'Liver-Eating' Johnston, Exploding the Myths – Discovering the Man," presents many of the known facts about Johnston's life.

xiv

Where there are gaps in the Johnston "timeline," authoritative speculation is offered to flesh-out Johnston's biographical "skeleton."

The wilderness experiences and exploits of John Johnston (a.k.a. John Garrison) were perhaps as impressive as were those of Jim Bridger and Kit Carson. Yet Johnston never achieved their level of fame and notoriety. This was apparently by design because he never purposefully sought the spotlight except but for one time - when he decided to join the Hardwick's "Great Rocky Mountain Wild West Show" in 1884 where he was billed (most appropriately) as The Avenging Fury of The Plains.

Johnston - A Man of Intrigue

To this day, Johnston remains a most fascinating frontier character. He possessed an amazing array of frontier skills and a remarkable gift for survival. His death at age 76 is proof of his wilderness abilities. His confidence in his marksmanship, his incredible strength, and his seemingly untiring energy levels, propelled him among the top ranks of the mountain men who plied their pelts in the early west.

This respected U.S. Army scout of the 1876-1877 Indian Wars spent most of his adult life in the wilderness. His life as a free trapper allowed him to live in the lap of the mountains, near beaver streams for quick access to his traps, near rifle and pistol and butcher knife in preparation for inevitable Sioux, Cheyenne or Blackfoot raiding parties.

Some Important Considerations

This book will detail a myriad of facts about the exploits of Johnston. It should delight most, and may, perhaps, sadden others. Some fans will view this book as breaking up the romance they enjoyed with the Johnston myth. This is quite understandable.

Conversely, to the reader with little or nor familiarity with the name of Liver-Eating Johnston, this book will serve as an excellent starting place in learning about the exploits that cast Johnston into the arms of myth and legend.

The Myth That Built Johnston's Reputation Never Happened!

The bottom line to remember is that John "Liver-Eating" Johnston was a sailor on board ship prior to, and during, the Mexican War of 1846-1847, when the Crow supposedly killed his pregnant Flathead wife.

The Crow were allies to both Johnston and the white race, despite the errant fables spun by Thorpe and Bunker in their novel, The Crow Killer.

Johnston stated time and time again that he was involved in over forty fights with the Indians from "California to the Gulf of Mexico." Never was the Crow nation involved. Why Thorpe and Bunker chose the Crow Nation to pick on for the supposed vendetta with Johnston has no basis in history. His battles were with the Blackfoot, Sioux, and Cheyenne – never the Crow.

It is hoped that *"The Avenging Fury of the Plains: John 'Liver-Eating' Johnston, Exploding the Myths – Discovering the Man,"* will answer many of the readers' questions about the life of Johnston. It is also hoped that this book will encourage the reader to perhaps conduct their own study and uncover more "Johnston gems" of historical truths that can add to the extant literature about John Johnston - certainly one of the most captivating characters of the old west

A
LIVER-EATING JOHNSTON
FACTOID

Johnston's Real Name was JOHN GARRISON

He was born in July of 1824 near Little York, New Jersey, the son of a poor farmer. Garrison purportedly changed his name after striking an officer on board ship during the Mexican War of 1846. True to his character, Johnston then jumped ship, and deserted

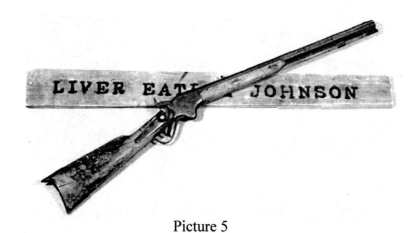

Picture 5
Johnston's Spenser Carbine.

1

Exploding the Myths

"If the American frontier did not exist,
it would have to be invented"
-Voltaire-

With the 1958 publishing of "Crow Killer: The Saga of Liver-Eating Johnson," by Thorpe and Bunker, Voltaire's prophecy was fulfilled. Their so-called Johnston "biography" was given flesh through the vivid imagination of Robert Bunker, the Crow Killer's primary author. Old "Jeremiah 'Liver- Eating'" Johnston was, indeed, invented.

For those who have previously read Thorpe and Bunker's book, you are soon be given a new perspective about the life of Johnston. Of course, for some, the fictional Liver-Eating Johnston will be just flat-out more fun and exciting than the real character. But the facts need to be made known.

In this chapter, I will present a summary of the primary myths penned by Thorpe and Bunker. These are the myths that created all the hype about the fictional Jeremiah Johnson character. Unfortunately, there are many gaps in the life of John Johnston. Much of the knowledge base that does exist emanates mostly from one source - Thorpe and Bunkers' novel.

Since they were the sole possessors of this "sacred knowledge" about the life of Johnston, they were deemed as authorities on the life of Johnston. Their readers did not know if what Thorpe and Bunker were writing about was fact or fiction. Their Crow Killer book became the point of reference for people seeking information about Johnston; hence, misinformation abounds.

Johnston's Presence in the Old West

Johnston was respected and feared by his Indian foe. His intelligence, strength, and fighting ability, sustained him during the years spent in the wilderness. Word spread that the Liver-Eater was "bad medicine." Similarly, Johnston commanded great respect from his peers — mountain men, trappers, and military superiors, for his competence in performing his duties and meeting the challenges of frontier life.

Yet, the name of John "Liver-Eating" Johnston is visibly absent from our American history books primarily because so little has been written about him. Nonetheless, his story remains one of fascination.

Many are intrigued by the compelling post-Civil War era that produced names like Sitting Bull, Crazy Horse, Chief Joseph, General Nelson A. Miles, and Yellowstone Kelly — men whose exploits have been forever etched in the collective minds of students of the early American west. It was to these self-same men to whom Johnston became connected, vis-à-vis, as scout in many hard-fought military campaigns during the great Indian Wars of 1876-1877.

The famous frontier scout, Yellowstone Kelly, with whom Johnston served under General Nelson A. Miles, stated in his autobiography that at the beginning of the Indian Wars in 1876-1877, Johnston was already recognized as a superior frontier presence. Kelly noted that among his scouts was, "...the celebrated hunter and frontiersman on whom rested the sobriquet of 'Liver-Eating Johnson.'" (1).

The "Crow Killer:" The Saga of Misinformation

Thorpe and Bunkers' book, "Crow Killer: The Saga of Liver-Eating Johnson,"(2) gives the reader an exhilarating look into the life of a fictitious mountain man named Jeremiah Johnson. However, there is very little truth found in the Crow Killer's one hundred ninety pages. A thimble-full of its contents has been proven verifiable.

For example, a hint about the ultimate veracity of the Crow Killer book is presented in the book's forward, offered by Richard M. Dorson. It states that, "...what we have here (Crow Killer) is the skeletal biography of a Rocky Mountain trapper and Indian fighter in the middle decades of the nineteenth century retold primarily on the basis of *word-of-mouth* sources." (italics mine). (3)

It is agreed that verbal exchanges and personal interviews can indeed help in fleshing out the skeletal biography of a man like Johnston. However, the problem lies in the fact that all we have are the authors' written records and their "personal interpretation" of the exploits and activities of Johnston.

It is now time to discuss the many inaccuracies found in the book, "Crow Killer," and to lay to rest the legends that have surrounded Johnston since his death in 1900.

MYTH BUSTING

In order to uncover the myths that yet surround the life of Johnston, it is necessary to evaluate the source of those myths – Thorpe and Bunker's *Crow Killer*. Following is a discussion of the *primary myths* that created the legendary life of Johnston. Other myths exist, but are simply too trivial to insert into this discussion; therefore, this author will focus on the myths that most contributed to the "question marks" inherent in Johnston's story.

The evidence employed to refute the tall tales of Thorpe and Bunker come from legitimate sources that can be found in the bibliography in the back of this book. The following summary includes the specific page in the Crow Killer book where the myths can be found.

MYTHS

1. *JOHNSTON MARRIED A FLATHEAD WOMAN NAMED THE "SWAN"*

Page 21: "One May morning in 1847, Crow Indians killed and scalped John Johnston's pregnant wife; for many years thereafter, he killed and scalped Crow Indians he ate their livers, raw." (4)

Reality

According to Johnston's June 12, 1884 military pension records (5) Johnston "was in the Navy." Other credible sources confirm Johnston's Mexican War experience. Rex Bundy, (6) J.X. Beidler, (7) and Will Carpenter (8) stated in their writings that Johnston arrived in the frontier at or about 1860 from the "coast" and that he was, indeed, a sailor. Various period newspapers also noted the same. Therefore, Johnston was not with the "Swan" because of his sea duties.

This key reality obliterates the message of the Crow Killer book. Since the bottom line is that Johnston was at sea during the time of the purported murder of his wife and child, the point in now *moot*.

Below is the reality about the relationship between the Crow Nation and the white race:

"The Crows not only tried to get along with the (whites) but fairly fawned on the Army." (9)

(Crimsoned Prairie: The Indian Wars)
S.L.A Marshall

There are many other evidences that could have been presented that clearly display the Crow nation's amicable

4

relationship with the whites. However, overkill is not necessary. Suffice it to say that Johnston's service in the Mexican War dismisses the fiction of Thorpe and Bunker.

2. *A TRAPPER NAMED DEL GUE WAS JOHNSTON'S PARTNER*

Page 22: "Johnston chose as his life-long partner a trapper Del Gue..." (10)

Years of research by this author has not located the name Del Gue in any *reliable* form of the written word, that has not been somehow been connected with the Thorpe and Bunker fable itself. As far as this researcher is aware, the only mention ever of Del Gue, other than in the *Crow Killer*, is in *"White Eye"* Anderson's book, "I Buried Hickok." Indeed, there may have been a frontiersman actually named Del Gue, but this author has not found evidence for it anywhere except for Anderson's book.

Since Thorpe and Bunker relied heavily upon White Eye Anderson's "interpretation' of his experiences with Del Gue in the Crow Killer, doubt is cast upon its historical truth.

Johnston did, however, have two actual partners (for a while) in John "X" Beidler, who was a vigilante, miner, and woodcutter; and Vic "Yellowstone" Smith, a famous buffalo hunter and frontier scout.

3. JOHNSTON ATE HUMAN LIVERS

Pg. 51: "...Crow warriors bodies – and only Crow warriors bodies – were found mutilated in special fashion: not merely scalped but cut beneath the ribs, and the livers removed. Del Gue, Bear Claw, and Bigfoot Davis... said Johnston was eating those livers." (11)

5

Reality

There are many accounts of how, and when, Liver-Eating Johnston earned his supposed reputation as a "cannibal." Exhaustive research has uncovered several timelines that attempt to place a firm date on exactly when it was that Johnston supposedly began to "devour" human livers. Most sources (except, of course, Thorpe and Bunker) place the date between 1868-1870. Only Thorpe and Bunker find Johnston sampling livers in the late 1840's, when Johnston was still onboard ship.

Documentation supporting the year 1868 as the year Johnston earned the name Liver-Eating, has been available for many years. Yet there remains a general vacuum, even among some authors, regarding accurate knowledge of how Johnston actually earned the name Liver-Eating.

The Liver-Eating episodes detailed below deal specifically with the *Sioux* – not the Crow. Although there are several accounts of how Johnston purportedly earned the name Liver-Eating Johnston, the following two accounts are the most accurate. A more in-depth account of this incident is described in another chapter.

Johnston was continually badgered during his life by the question "did you really eat a piece of a man's liver?" Typically, Johnston's retort was always that the story was, indeed, *a joke*. Let's look below and examine the two reports that best summarizes the truth about Johnston's mythical liver-eating proclivities.

Billings Times, July 27, 1899

This first account of how Johnston received the name "Liver-Eating" was reported six months prior to Johnston's death in January 1900. Johnston was at the famous Hunter's Hot Springs trying to get some relief from his rheumatism.

Johnston knew that he was dying. He suffered from an assortment of medical problems that made life almost unbearable for him. One day, a young reporter asked Johnston if ever did actually eat Crow liver. Johnston adamantly stated:

"It's a domd (sic) lie. I know I got that reputation, but `tain't so. I'll tell how 'twas. It was at the head of the Musselshell. It was back in '68. There was 15 of us and we were hunting and making a wood camp. We was attacked by Injuns, and we licked `em – licked 'em good. Hairy Bear was the name of their chief. We killed 36 of them and wounded 60. I chased down one Indian... then I scalped him... then I ran my knife into him and killed him and part of his liver came out with the knife. I waved the knife with the liver on it in the air and yelled 'Come on, and have a piece! It'll stay yer' stomach 'till you get home to dinner.'"(12)

The Pioneer Press, December 21, 1884

The second version of how Johnston "earned" his name comes to us from a letter published in a newspaper by an unnamed officer of the 7th Cavalry. This officer, under whom Johnston served as scout during the Nez Perce war of 1877, explains how he personally heard Johnston describe the method by which he earned the name Liver-Eating:

"...(I) saw one buck tumble from his pony and crawl into the brush, so I went after him. Putting my knife into him, I gave it a turn. And when I pulled it out, there was a piece of liver sticking to the knife. So I held it up and yelled to the fellow next to me, 'say Jim, won't you have a bite?' That's all there is to the story. Some say I ate it, but it's a lie." (13)

(Unknown 7th Cavalry Officer's Comments)

4.   JOHN JOHNSTON DIDN'T DRINK

Pg. 64:   "Thirty-six scalps were like money in the
bank and Liver-Eating Johnston was a
thrifty man, with no merely conventional
vices. Once home, he doffed his new Crow
white skin suit and put on old and greasy
skins. He never drank." (14)

Reality

Thorpe and Bunker portray Johnston as a sympathetic
figure that is somehow justified in punishing those responsi-
ble for supposed murdering his "Flathead" wife. After all,
how can Johnston think clearly if his resolve is diluted with
whiskey!

"During steamboat days on the Missouri, the Liver-
Eater would stand along the river and watch the
boats. His costume consisted of one shirt, ballooned
up by the wind, and a whiskey-soaked, burr- matted
beard..." (15)   (High Border Country)
                              Eric Thane

A Bizarre Johnston Drinking Episode

Johnston friend, Burt Marvin, recorded the following
drinking episode involving Johnston. It was later discussed
during a lecture by Ann Fendrich (Park County Historical
Society):

"Burt told how Johnston sobered up after one of
the drinking binges he went on every three or four
months. He would get a chicken, a big pot, a quart
of whiskey and a barrel. He would then go down to
the river. There he cooked the chicken until it fell
to pieces in the pot. Then he would drink a little
soup, have some of his whiskey and roll over the

barrel. He kept this up as long as the chicken soup and the whiskey lasted. When he was done with that, he was sober." (16)

More Problems With Alcohol in 1872 Fort Benton:

"Although 'Liver-Eating' Johnson has achieved considerable notoriety by reason of his career in Montana, and was admittedly, a courageous and resourceful frontiersman when occasion required, as a matter of fact his reputation at many of the early-day forts and settlements was that of a drunken bum - he was drunk most of the time. But even in that capacity he seems to have done good for the settlers." (17)   R.M. Husbandman

5.   JOHNSTON TOOK SCALPS DURING THE CIVIL WAR

Scalping during the Civil War indeed did occur. Indians serving on the North and the South were generally the ones performing the gruesome deeds (although some whites did take scalps from their Indian enemies). While it is true that many accounts exist about Johnston taking scalps from his Indian foe in the wilderness, there is absolutely no proof in his Army records that Johnston got in trouble for I during the Civil War.

Pgs. 90-91: "John Johnston...took a vast harvest of Seminole and Cherokee scalps. But while the Seminoles were Confederate soldiers, these Cherokees fought for the Union. Reprimanded sharply, the Crow Killer gave up his booty and longed for the wilderness." (18)

Reality

Johnston's military records note only one military breach; when he decided to desert from Benton Barracks, St. Louis, Missouri, *five days* after he arrived for duty. To his credit, Johnston did return to camp voluntarily. Below is his desertion record from the 2nd Colorado Company Descriptive Book:

Descriptive List of Deserters - John Johnson

Dated:	Near St. Louis, Mo: February 29, 1864
Age:	33 years (Johnston lied – he was 39
Height:	5 feet 11 ^{1}/2 inches
Complexion:	Light
Hair:	Brown
Eyes:	Hazel
Enlisted:	February 24, 1864
Where:	St. Louis, Mo
Period:	3 years
Deserted:	February 29, 1864
Where:	Benton Barracks
Remarks:	Returned without being apprehended (2nd Colorado Company Descriptive Book)

Johnston's military records tell us nothing in-depth about his punishment for desertion. His record does label him a "straggler," which is simply another way of stating that Johnston was, indeed, a deserter.

6. JOHNSTON GUIDED "PORTUGEE" PHILLIPS TO FORT LARAMIE

The fable about Johnston guiding "Portugee" Phillips to within twenty miles of Fort Laramie to announce the horrific news that Lt. Colonel William Fetterman, and his entire force of eighty-one soldiers, were massacred by the Sioux, is romantic, but false.

> Pg. 101: (Event: Phillips rides into the Johnston and Beidler camp, exhausted).
>
> "Johnston lifted him (Phillips) from the saddle "as gently as if he had been a baby... "(19)
>
> Pg. 101: "I'll just show Portygee over the rough parts". (20)

REALITY

The amazing ride by Phillip's from Fort Kearny to Fort Laramie in December of 1866 was accomplished in horrid weather conditions. Phillips also had to battle lack of sleep, the threat of Sioux attacks, the risk of injury, and concern for the strength and endurance of his borrowed horse.

The truth regarding this incident is that Johnston had nothing to do with Phillips' ride. Another rider aided Phillips, but it *was not* Johnston:

"Less well known is that Carrington (Fort Kearny commander) sent out another volunteer messenger from the fort, George Bailey, who also made it through the blizzards and hostile Native Americans, meeting up with Phillips sometime before Horse Shoe Station. Both men arrived together at the telegraph office and later at Fort Laramie."(21)

11

Another source has also reported that someone other than Johnston aided Phillips in his ride to Fort Laramie:

"The famous ride of John 'Portugee' Phillips to Fort Laramie to take the news of the Fetterman disaster of Dec. 21, 1866, was remarkable but it appears he did not ride alone. Carrington's scrapbook, now in the Wyoming Room at the Sheridan County Fulmer Public Library, indicates Carrington sent two men, Phillips and Dixon, to the telegraph office at Horseshoe Station, and historian Robert A. Murray shows that two men were paid ($300.00) for the trip. Phillips then rode into Fort Laramie alone." (22)

Fort Phil Kearny
Bozeman Trail Association and Foundation

One final look:

"Legend tells us that Colonel Carrington's thoroughbred horse dropped dead as Phillips dismounted at the door of *Old Bedlam* (the name of the building at Fort Laramie where a Christmas party was underway). He had good reason. So long a ride in only four days – the night of December 21 (1866) to the night of December 25 – would be fantastic even in good weather and daylight. Phillips had neither, although he may have changed horses somewhere along the way- at Horse Shoe Station, perhaps." (23)

(The Bloody Bozeman)
Dorothy M. Johnson

Picture 6
Fort Laramie's Old Bedlam in 1875.
This is the building where Portugee Phillips delivered the
news of the Fetterman disaster.

7. JOHNSTON FRIEND, MARIANO MODENO, KILLED UTE CHIEF, CAPTAIN JACK

In a marvelous piece of writing on *page 147*, Thorpe and Bunker present their interpretation about the grisly death of Captain Jack.

"The gaunt outlines of a giant cottonwood towered there. The cold breeze hissed among the dry leaves remaining on its branches. Far overhead a limb, bent slightly at its outer end, held the swinging body of an Indian, held hand and foot with rawhide. He had not been hanged by the neck but on plaited rope of rawhide passed beneath his arms and knotted at the back. That he was still alive, the twitchings of his body could attest. That he was still conscious his direct gaze attested, from black, hate-filled eyes.

His lips uttered not a sound. Captain Jack dying in agony was still Captain Jack, the Ute chief." (24)

REALITY

The reality is that there **was no** Mariano Modeno. There was, however, a *Mariano Medina*, from Colorado, who similarly fought the Utes. The truth about the fate of Captain Jack is found below. Thorpe and Bunkers' insistence on "throwing Mariano Modeno" into Captain Jack's life is another case of how Thorpe and Bunker once again fractured the truth in the narration below:

"Chief Jack, the most intelligent of the White River Utes, refused to go to the Uintah Reservation, preferring to become a teamster on the Rawlins/Fort Washakie Road. On April 29, 1882, the Fort Washakie commander, Major J.W. Mason, sent Lt. George Morgan, Sergeant Casey and 5 privates, to a nearby Indian village to arrest Jack for questioning about a horse theft. Jack declined to surrender and was wounded in the arm as he ducked into a tepee. When the soldiers pulled down the tepee, Jack ran into another, 'well-filled with bales of robes and raw hides by which he was well protected from our bullets.' During attempts to pull down the second tepee, Jack fired and killed Sgt. Casey. Major Mason arrived then, and, in his own words 'upon learning the condition of affairs, I caused a shell from a mountain howitzer to be fired into the tepee in which Ute Jack was, killing him.'"(25)

(Massacre: The Tragedy at White River)
Marshall Sprague

14

Picture 7
UTE CHIEF, CAPTAIN JACK
Captain Jack (Standing, Upper Left)

Thorpe and Bunker state in their novel that Captain
Jack died at the hands of the fictitious character
Mariano Medeno. Captain Jack certainly recovered
nicely to have his picture taken in later years.

Picture 8
MARIANO MEDINA

This little guy, Mariano Medina, is the true
frontiersman Thorpe and Bunker picked-on to
turn into "Mariano Medeno." Imagine this vicious hombre trying to lift Captain Jack into a
tree, to string him up?

8. JOHNSTON NEVER SAW A "NEGRO"

Pg, 157: "Now the legend has it that Johnson was curious, having never seen a Negro before, and indeed he likely had seen none since coming west." (26)

Johnston purportedly sought gold in California prior to his entrance into Montana Territory. If this is true, then Johnston definitely saw African Americans among the miners when he purportedly was mining gold in Sutter's Fort, California because,

"early in the (gold) rush, San Francisco, Sacramento, Marysville, and Stockton all had clearly identifiable black communities, and mining locations had names reflecting the presence of one – and usually more – African Americans: Negro Bar, Negro Hill, Negro Slide, Negro Tent, Negro Flat..." (27)

Johnston in the Mexican War

As with every war in which America was involved, African-Americans fought side-by-side with white soldiers. It was the same with the U.S. Navy. Johnston definitely encountered African-Americans as:

"...about 1000 black sailors served on U.S. ships during the Mexican War...on ships blockading ports of entry (the Caribbean and Pacific Oceans) during the war." (28)

Johnston in the Civil War

Johnston served with the 2nd Colorado Cavalry during the Civil War from February 24, 1864 to September 23, 1865. African-American men, serving with the 2nd, 3rd, and 4th Missouri Infantry units, trained alongside Johnston at Benton Barracks, St. Louis. (29)

Picture 9
African-American Troops at Benton Barracks

Thorpe and Bunker stated that Johnston never saw an African-American. Yet, these young, strong, African American troops trained alongside Liver-Eating Johnston at Benton Barracks, in St. Louis, Missouri.

9. JOHNSTON FRIEND, MUGGINS TAYLOR, WAS JOHNSTON'S DEPUTY

Pg. 179: "Henry Lumpp, drunk, shot, and killed Johnston's deputy-helper, Muggins Taylor." (30)

REALITY

Muggins Taylor was not Johnston's deputy-helper as Thorpe and Bunker wrote. Taylor was Coulson, Montana's second deputy sheriff. Johnston was Justice of the Peace of Custer County at the same time Taylor was serving as sheriff.

May 1882: "After the good people of Coulson petitioned for a Deputy, H.M. (Muggins) Taylor was appointed deputy sheriff by Tom Irvine of Miles City, sheriff of Custer County." (31)

Oct. 1882: "After 'Muggin's Taylor's death, John ('Liver-Eating') Johnston [Johnson] became one of the county deputies." (32)

10. JOHNSTON WOULD NEVER JOIN A WILD WEST SHOW

Thorpe and Bunker tell us that Johnston *would never join up with a Wild West show:*

Pg. 187: "...Nor would he (Johnston) move East for the fat offers made him by Buffalo Bill; Doc W. F. Carver, though he had originated such shows himself, laughed at the very idea of Liver-Eating Johnson leaving the West that was his" (33)

Reality

"On August 16, 1884, the Livingston paper noted, 'The Calamity Jane - Liver-Eating Johnson - Crow Indian - Cowboy combination called Hardwick's show, busted in Chicago. The members of the circus were not paid by the manager and were forced to sell their ponies in order to get back to Montana." (34) (Pieces & Places of Billings History: Local Markers and Sites)

Joyce M. Jensen

An End to the Johnston Myths

The reader now knows the truth about the various myths that surrounded Johnston's life. The remaining chapters in this book will provide a solid summary of the key events that shaped Johnston's life.

A
LIVER-EATING JOHNSTON
FACTOID

Legend Tells Us That Liver-Eating
Johnston Stood <u>6' 6"</u>.
In Truth, Johnston was 5' 11½".

2

The Silence of the Lion: The Early Years

1824-1862

On a warm July day in 1824, a mile or so from the village of Little York, New Jersey, a boy was born to Isaac and Eliza-Metlar Garrison. (35) According to the late Harry Owens, of Red Lodge, Montana, Johnston had five sisters, the last of which, Matilda Tillman, died in Rochester, New York, in 1923.

There has been some discussion regarding the idea that Johnston had a brother who died in Virginia during the Civil War, as per Isaac Garrison's pension information. This is where Johnston's family dynamics gets interesting, if not confusing.

Researcher Dorman Nelson believes that Liver-Eating Johnston's *brother* was named _John_ and that Liver-Eating Johnston's true birth name was really _William_. Nelson believes that Liver-Eating Johnston may have "jumped ship in 1858," changed his name to _John Johnston_, and eventually landed in the Montana gold fields in 1862.

Regardless of the apparent Garrison family conundrum, the important point here is that progress is being made in uncovering interesting gems about the life of Johnston that have, heretofore, been hiding in plain sight. May it continue.

The Vacuum That Is Johnston's Early Life

Little else is known of Liver-Eating Johnston's youth and teenage years, or of the activities in which he participated. It is a safe bet to state that the harshness and apparent brutalities afflicted by Johnston's father, Isaac, on the young John "Garrison" Johnston, probably prompted Johnston to leave New Jersey forever; for there is no evidence that he ever returned home to at any time for a visit.

But sadly, with no knowledge of his youth, our only guide to evaluate the life of Johnston is by his deeds as an adult. From perhaps an innocent youth, Johnston would eventually metamorphose into an angry, explosively lethal young man, clearly capable of violent acts. Yet it was precisely this very quality that gained him entrance into the most exclusive western fraternity of all – that of the rock-hard, highly competent, frontiersman.

When destiny finally transported Johnston into, and among, the dangers of the wilderness, Johnston had little apparent problems making the adjustment. An alcoholic father who nearly worked him to death had apparently toughened him. It's quite obvious that there was a grizzly bear size rage festering inside Johnston most of the time.

Johnston and the Open Seas

Liver-Eating Johnston's first recorded adventure was his apparent employment on a whaling vessel. In a February 7, 1900 newspaper article (two weeks after Johnston's death) mention was made of the various enterprises entered into by Johnston, including his experience as a whaler:

"John Johnson was born in New Jersey 77 years ago (it was actually 76), and was of Irish descent (probably Scottish/German). In his early days he shipped on a whaling vessel..." (36)

In an article written by Will Carpenter in 1971, it was noted that "...Johnston was a lad of sixteen, and working on a coastal schooner on the East Coast." (37)

It is probable that Johnston made the decision to leave his family to escape the "bond-servant" role cast upon him by his father, Isaac Garrison. Isaac would send his young son to local farmers to work off his (Isaac's) debts. Perhaps Johnston was infatuated with the idea of sailing the high seas

– the apparent, and ultimate, escape. Not a few hardy young men decided to actualize the romance of the high seas.

Maybe the riveting stories told by sea captains about the dangers of hunting the great leviathan undoubtedly intrigued impressionable young minds like Johnston with things mysterious. Alternatively, as commented upon earlier, it may have all boiled down to a simple formula - escape the oppressive life he lived under a debauched father.

During the 1830's and 1840's, many whaling companies flourished along New Jersey's Atlantic Ocean seacoast. Businesses such as the Newark Whaling, Sealing and Manufacturing Company hired men for its Newark, New Jersey, depot. One of the ships that docked in Newark was the "Whaling Ship John Wells." It was not unusual for a whaling voyage to remain out to sea for up to three years.

On one trip, for example, the ship John Wells was afloat from July 20, 1841 to May 9, 1844. It sailed around Cape Horn, South America; its destination – the Northwest coast of current Oregon and Washington. (38)

Similarly, other whaling companies sailed out of New Jerseys' Cape May and Long Beach Island. Perhaps Johnston signed on board ship in Philadelphia, which was only forty-five miles from Johnston's home in Western New Jersey.

Unfortunately, no record exists as for which company Johnston may have worked. But at least history does record that Johnston apparently spent time as a whaler.

It was obvious that whaling did not provide enough adventure for Johnston. The boredom and tedium on board ship must have been particularly difficult for Johnston to endure. However, it was clear that the high seas continued to figure in his plans. Therefore, leaving his brief sea faring career in his "wake," Johnston enlisted in the U.S. Navy during the Mexican War.

Johnston's First Taste of Naval Battle

It is not known precisely when Johnston enlisted as a seaman, but Union Army enlistment records, as well as

24

period newspapers, reported that Johnston did serve aboard ship.

The Carbon County Democrat reported in 1900 that:

"... after a few voyages (aboard a whaling ship) Johnston enlisted in the United States Navy, and was in the service during the Mexican War." (39)

A search of the Unites States Archives in Washington, DC, produced a few tantalizing leads about the possible identity of a sailor named John Garrison who served upon a Philadelphia-based frigate named the *Raritan* during the Mexican War. However, this is pure speculation and cannot be verified as being the character we are seeking to locate.

The Mexican War Begins

The Mexican War began in May 1846 as a result of America's expansionist policy. In March of 1845, Congress voted to annex the Republic of Texas and make it the Lone Star State. Mexico believed this to be a hostile act. At the same time, President Polk was making a bid to annex California from the Mexicans and offered Mexico a large sum of money in compensation. But the Mexicans flatly refused to exchange land for money.

Because Mexico had no interest in giving up Texas, Polk ordered troops into Texas to advance as far as the Rio Grande and seize the disputed area. On April 25, 1846, (ten years after the Alamo) Mexican soldiers, and a party of American cavalrymen, clashed. Several Americans were killed. When this news reached Washington, it gave Polk an excuse for a fight.

Johnston – The Mexican War Deserter

Liver-Eating Johnston's weak character was displayed on board ship during the Mexican American War. It was similarly displayed during the Civil War, as the reader will discover later in the book. Johnston was clearly an impulsive, hardened man, who apparently had a dangerously short fuse. Historical accounts about Johnston tend not to mention accounts of Johnston's brutalities against his Indian foe, his reluctance to discuss his past, his whiskey drinking, his desire to purposefully and joyously shock the sensibilities of others, his isolation, sullenness, and great restlessness, that was manifested during his lifetime

It is not known how long Johnston served aboard ship as a sailor. But it obviously was not an extended period of time because Johnston's temper got the best of him. Remember, researcher Dorman Nelson states that Johnston was still sailing the seas up until 1858 (perhaps under the name of William Garrison (?). We don't know for certain if it was with the US Navy or a merchant ship.

The Reason Johnston Deserted the US Navy

A fascinating revelation from a 1900 newspaper article discusses an incident that occurred aboard the vessel upon which Johnston served during the Mexican War. This incident apparently was the trigger point that forced Johnston to jump ship. It is obvious that Johnston exploded into rage onboard ship as he witnessed his comrade being struck by the lieutenant in charge. This fact about Johnston's naval experience is representative of Johnston's lack of self-control. The following excerpt details the incident:

"The only incident he (Johnston) related of his naval experience was an act of insubordination, which was to his credit. A lieutenant, son of a commodore, struck one of his comrades a bad blow with his sword, when young Johnston dealt the officer a stunning blow in the neck, stretching him senseless on the deck. The officer, when he came to, did not know whether he had been struck by lightning or one of the spars, but Johnston was suspected. None would testify against him, however, so he escaped the capital punishment that would have been his fate, but was regarded with such suspicion that for thirty days he got no shore leave. When he did finally to go ashore for one day he never returned and drifted to the unknown west." (40)

It is interesting that the *lieutenant suspected Johnston.* Why? One can only imagine what trouble Johnston caused on board ship prior to the incident with the lieutenant. The consequences of striking a commanding officer during the Mexican War were, indeed, severe.

A major part of the problem with which a sailor had to deal was the day-by-day boredom associated with running blockades and preventing goods and reinforcements from reaching the Mexican Army. Johnston apparently lacked the discipline to deal with his difficult situation on board ship.

Johnston was extremely fortunate that he was not apprehended and charged with this serious offence. An example of what could have happened to Johnston is detailed below:

"Seaman Samuel Jackson had loosed a torrent of abuse and twice struck the officer of the deck in an altercation over Jackson's shoes being on deck after an inspection. He was court-martialed on a variety of charges including striking an officer, and sentenced to be hanged. The sentence was carried out during the morning of September 17, 1846." (41)

Red Lodge, Montana's, Harry Owens

In discussions with the late Johnston historian, Harry Owens of Red Lodge, Montana, Owens divulged that Johnston's real name was Garrison. Owens was the first to discover that Johnston also had five sisters in New Jersey.

As the character of Johnston is gradually revealed to the reader, there is yet another incident which provides a small window into Johnston's life. When Johnston enlisted in the Union Army, he lied about his age. Was he afraid that his past Mexican War desertion would catch up with him? His

Civil War records state that he was thirty-three years of age at the time of his enlistment (1864). But since he was born in July of 1824, Johnston was actually thirty-nine.

It was known that Johnston was seventy-six years at the time of death in 1900. (42) His death certificate verified that he was indeed seventy-six years of age when he died in the Veterans Hospital in Los Angeles, California.

Owens was confident that Johnston's actual name was John "Garrison." Johnston had confided his secret to a close friend and fellow pioneer, John Webber, when Johnston was dying.

Owens was in possession of a 1937 newspaper interview of John Webber that stated that Liver-Eating Johnston's true name was John Garrison. Since Owens was a life-long resident of Red Lodge, Montana, the town where Johnston lived for approximately twelve years until the time of his death, Owens was quite familiar with the intimate stories and anecdotes that still fill the streets of Red Lodge even today.

An interesting side note is that Harry Owens' uncle, Fred Longmore, was one of the young men who escorted Johnston to the train in December of 1899 as Johnston was about to leave for the Veteran's hospital in California. Owens did, indeed, have an "insiders" view of what occurred during the lifetime of Liver-Eating Johnston.

As was discussed earlier, the most logical motivation for Garrison changing his name to Johnston is obvious. When he decided to desert from his ship, Johnston knew he was a fugitive on the run. If caught, he (Garrison) risked the chance of death by hanging.

As was earlier mentioned, there is speculation that when Johnston "jumped ship" in 1858, he changed his name from William (?) Garrison to John Johnston.

Again, despite the lack of solid evidence, it matters little. There is ample proof that Johnston spent much of his youth at sea, after which, he eventually planted his feet on solid ground in the Montana gold fields of 1862.

A Man's Name Can Get Him Hung

Johnston himself gave us a clear hint about his almost whimsical attitude about changing names, as was reported by a Helena (Montana) Independent newspaper reporter. Johnston reportedly stated to friends "nobody cared what a man's name was before he left home." (43)

That Johnston told a few close friends his real name tells us that he waited until the right time for him to feel safe to disclose his true name. To make certain, Harry Owens hired an expert to search his ancestry back in New Jersey. That's when Harry confirmed that Johnston did, indeed, have several sisters, and that he was, truly, one of the Garrison's from Little York, New Jersey. Owens found no brother.

However, Liver-Eating Johnston's father had three different women who bore him children. Therefore, one can speculate that other children were born into the Garrison family. Further research is needed to solidify Johnston's family tree.

Stepping Onto California Soil

There is no record of exactly where Johnston took his shore leave when he *deserted from the Navy*. But all indications lead to California. An article by Rex Bundy stated that Johnston "jumped ship in San Francisco and went to the California mining districts." (44)

However, Bundy had Johnston arriving to California in 1860 – twelve years after the end of the Mexican War. Perhaps Bundy was referring to the period around 1858 when Johnston departed from the ship to which he was attached, as was suggested by Dorman Nelson. But, in all probability, we will never know for certain. Regardless of the uncertainty, Bundy's article helps to clarify that Johnston may have left his ship and stepped onto California soil in San Francisco.

Another hint given to us by Johnston's old friend and drinking cohort, J.X. Beidler (of Montana Vigilante fame), tells us in his memoirs that "he (Johnston) came from the coast... and being exceptionally expert with his rifle was soon known as a bad man to impose on." (45)

The American Army and Navy Seize California

Although peace was declared with Mexico in September 1847, the war was not over until 1848; but to the victor goes the spoils. California was now under the flag of the United States. If, indeed, Johnston did desert, he apparently left ship before the war was officially over.

As a seaman, Johnston and his shipmates undoubtedly spent most of their time blockading the Mexican coastlines on two oceans (Pacific and Gulf of Mexico). It was a thankless, but vital, service. So perhaps Johnston's duties onboard simply bored him and triggered his burgeoning fury, causing him to strike the lieutenant.

In trying to set an approximate date for when Johnston could have possibly deserted to California soil from his ship, a chronological summary of when the U.S. forces took possession of major California coast cities is pertinent to the Johnston timeline.

The US Navy and Army entered the following cities, as victors in 1847, on the following dates:

Monterey...............July 7,
San Francisco..........July 9,
San Diego..............July 29,
Santa Barbara..........August 4,
Los Angeles............August 13,

If, as Rex Bundy stated in his article, Johnston "jumped ship" in San Francisco, then it had to have been after July 9,

1847. If Johnston deserted in 1847, he would have been twenty-three years of age.

Dreams in the Rivers: Gold Prospecting

Rex Bundy reported that after Johnston deserted, he eventually joined the gold rush as a prospector. Like others, he wanted to strike it rich. It wasn't until January 1848, that the first gold strike occurred at John Sutter's Fort, the site of which is now part of the city of Sacramento. Interestingly, a fellow New Jerseyan by the name of James Marshall (who lived only about twenty-minutes from Johnston in New Jersey) was the man who discovered gold at Sutter's Fort.

If the assumption is that San Francisco was indeed Johnston's city of entry into California, and if the time period for his departure date was July-August of 1847 is correct, then we can also assume that Johnston did, eventually, participate in the madness of searching for gold, approximately six months after he decided to desert from the Navy. Regardless, Johnston continued to pursue gold prospecting for much of his life, apparently never finding enough gold to make his efforts worthwhile.

Sutter's Fort had become a magnet for a variety of people, and became known as a location where men of similar pursuits gathered to trade and drink. Sutter's Fort, "quickly became the rendezvous for all the trappers, hunters and wandering people of all sorts in the surrounding territory, besides the emigrants who came from the East over the Oregon Trail, the Fort being its terminal." (46)

The Conflict Between Native Americans and Miners

Liver-Eating Johnston once said in a letter that he had been in "forty different Indian fights, and fought them from California to the Gulf of Mexico."(47) It is likely that Johnston's stay in California could have introduced him to "Indian" fighting.

Once gold was discovered in Sutter's Fort, a huge migration of miners made their way to the mining site. The effect upon the indigenous Indian was profound because the United States decided to adopt a policy declaring that when gold was found on Indian land, the Indians had to be extracted from their tribal homes. An 1849 statement by U.S. Army's General Carleton callously defined the new policy:

> "The miners will go to their country (Native Americans), and the question which comes up is, shall the miners be protected and the country be developed, or shall the Indians be suffered to kill them and the nation be deprived of its immense wealth?" (48)

As new mining sites were developed, the Indians were pushed further back and forced to move away from their traditional homelands. Despite harsh treatment, they rarely troubled a mining camp.

However, the Indians did attack stagecoach lines, wagon trains containing emigrants, and supply trains, and generally caused trouble in order to indirectly "get back" at the miners. The Indians did not typically attack mining camps because they considered miners to be "bad medicine."

California Begins To Populate

The population of white settlers in 1847-1850 California was principally composed of three groups. The *first group* was composed of *mountain men and free trappers*; men who typically identified with the local Indian and often resided in their encampments.

The *second* assemblage of settlers was the *desperados, murderers* and *thieves*. These men continually robbed, killed and thoroughly intimidated travelers seeking to strike it rich. The treachery had reached such terrible proportions that vigilante committees were developed to handle the situation. The *third group* was the ordinary citizen of good character. This group made up the largest of the three types populating California during the gold rush era. (49)

Of all groups, Johnston probably fell in with the mountain men and trappers, although he seemed to have a proclivity for untoward characters. It is reasonable to conclude that Liver-Eating Johnston was tutored by his new comrades concerning the rigors and challenges of the wilderness.

No Major Wars

Although the Native Americans were treated badly and were dispossessed from their homes, they did not retaliate on a grand scale. There were occasional skirmishes between miner and Indian, but these incidents never led to war.

One of these skirmishes occurred at Mormon Island. A miner became involved with the wife of an Indian chief. When the chief complained, he was killed. There was some retaliation by the Native Americans about this incident, which resulted in death on both sides. But the hostilities were only brief, and resulted in the Native Americans moving further into the mountains.

Could Johnston have gotten involved with some of these feuds? Since he reported that he had fought Native Americans in California, there is an excellent probability that, as a miner, Johnston became introduced to Indian warfare. By the time gold was discovered at Sutter's Fort, there were approximately 20,000 indigenous Native Americans in California. (50)

However, the tremendous influx of emigrants, miners and seekers of dreams, swelled the populated regions of California, quickly outnumbering the indigenous population. Perhaps Liver-Eating Johnston began to feel too "crowded in," frustrated because he had not made his fortune. Perhaps he moved on to more remote regions in other territories that provided him elbowroom in order to pursue gold prospecting and trapping.

A
LIVER-EATING JOHNSTON
FACTOID

A FORMIDABLE WEAPON

Johnston's Sharps buffalo rifle was basically a
"needle gun," which fired a bullet shaped like a
great spike, using 120 grains of powder to propel
it through the body of any foe who crossed
his path.

3

Dreams In the Rivers: Gold Fever

The pages of American History from 1840 to 1862 finds little reference to Liver-Eating Johnston. As has been earlier discussed, Johnston spent his "early years" at sea–probably until about 1858. To earn a living after his tenure as a seaman concluded, Johnston apparently trapped beaver, hunted buffalo and pursued wolfing - and fought Indians. However, by the time Johnston stepped into the rivers with his beaver traps, the beaver trade had all but died out.

The beaver, whose pelts were called "hairy banks notes," had been previously trapped out in the best beaver streams by the end of the 1830's. The beaver hat, once in great demand by both Americans and Europeans, was eventually replaced by trendy headgear of silk and other materials. Beaver pelts, also called "plews," once garnered as much as five dollars apiece. But the eventual decrease in demand drastically dropped the price to one dollar. Johnston still trapped beaver even into the late 1870's and sold his pelts to local trading posts.

The sale of buffalo robes quickly replaced beaver. It is known that Liver-Eating Johnston was a buffalo hunter, providing food for the Army, especially for the soldiers in Fort Laramie, Wyoming, as well as obtaining buffalo robes for sale or trade.

Johnston needed to trade his hides for goods and supplies, a necessary enterprise for survival. He needed to obtain blankets, lead for bullets, tobacco, cloth, various implements and ornaments in order to make it through the year.

Although not much is known of Johnston's whereabouts during the late 1840's and 1850's, with the exception of his being "on the seas," he undoubtedly earned a living by hunting and trading. It is also safe to state that Johnston lived with various friendly Indian tribes from time to time.

Mining in Colorado and Montana

As has been ascertained, it is reasonable to conclude that Johnston traversed the virgin territories of western United States to seek gold. It is not known how long Johnston remained in California, ultimately settling in Montana after gold mining in Colorado ran its course.

He may have followed other fortune hunters to the Colorado mining camps such as Cherry Creek, and then perhaps to Dry Gulch and Pikes Peak in 1859.

It has been reported that many of these self-same miners from the Pikes Peak gold strike later joined the 2nd Colorado Cavalry during the Civil War to fight for the Union against the likes of William Quantrill, "Bloody Bill" Anderson and Confederate troops commanded by General Sterling Price.

The 2nd Colorado Cavalry Volunteers thus fought in both Kansas and Missouri, where

"...the Colorado boys could test their courage against Missouri bushwhackers-a savory assignment for Pikes Peak prospectors who had survived among wild Utes and Arapaho." (51)

The Cheyenne, Arapaho, and Utes

During the fervency of Colorado gold strikes, the indigenous Indians proved to be extremely compliant with their oft-times bad treatment by the whites. The reason that there was little conflict was because the whites generally chose to live in areas away from the territory of the mountain tribes and those of the plains.

The Native Americans wanted to maintain a good relationship with the whites because the whites provided arms and ammunition that would be used against other enemy tribes with who they were in constant conflict.

It wasn't until 1864 (Liver-Eating Johnston was already in Missouri during the Civil War) when open hostilities developed between the whites and the Indians, which quickly escalated into warfare as a result of the Fort Wise treaty.

The Southern Cheyenne and the Arapahos ceded most of their land and were duped by a questionable clause in the treaty that allowed a railroad to cut through their land. The once peaceful Native Americans could tolerate no more lies. Open hostilities had erupted and the Colorado/Kansas war had begun.

Johnston Moves on to Montana Territory

Liver-Eating Johnston apparently never did find gold in Colorado. There were occasional rumors of gold in the south central and southwestern part of Montana, so it seems that Johnston decided to make a move north to unknown parts.

A credible piece of evidence exists that tells us what Liver-Eating Johnston did to carve out a living in the Big Sky Country when he arrived there in or about 1860:

"Traveling alone or in pairs (frontiersman), they were in constant danger from wild beasts, or the savage Indians and usually sooner or later they met a swift death, fortunate if a companion escaped to bring back tidings of their death. Years afterward some other wanderer might stumble upon their bleaching bones and bring back word of their fate. But among them were now and then men of unusual strength and wit to cope with the wild surroundings and of such was 'Liver-Eating Johnson.' He had hairbreadth escapes and saw companions ambushed at his side. During the years after 1860 (there were) periods of intense warfare of Sioux and Cheyenne against the invading plainsmen. Johnson took part in the Bozeman expeditions, the trouble in Fort Pease and other conflicts between Indians and armed civilians." (52)

It is readily apparent that Johnston's warfare with Native Americans had begun in earnest as he moved about the mountains and plains of Wyoming and Montana. It certainly must have been to his liking because he chose to live in Montana from 1865 (after his discharge from the Army) until December of 1899, when he left for California to enter the National Soldiers Home in Los Angeles, California, where he died a month later.

Yellow Treasure in Bannack and Alder Gulch, Montana Territory

A 1922 Helena, Montana newspaper article recalled the time when Johnston began prospecting for gold in Montana. The article stated that Johnston traveled to principally two towns in order to seek his fortune.

It was reported that Johnston "was among the first gold seekers to come to Bannack and Alder Gulch for a few months, (then) he went to Colorado..." (53) In all probability, Johnston did not journey directly to Colorado to enlist in the Army. If Johnston had enlisted in the U.S. Army from Colorado, his records would have reflected that he joined up in either of these Colorado "Camps": *Denver, Collins, Curtis, Fillmore, Robbins, Weld, and/or Cannon City.* His military records do not reflect the above newspaper articles' supposition. Indeed, Johnston may have left Alder Gulch later than was reported to enlist at St. Louis, Missouri.

The manner in which gold was discovered in Bannack is a fascinating story. It also shows us how quickly Johnston moved to get into the gold mining district as soon as he heard the news.

On July 28, 1862, two prospectors from Colorado, named John White and John McGavin, discovered one of the largest gold strikes in the west. The men were camped in the Beaverhead Valley, south of Lewis and Clark's passage, in Montana Territory, near the current Idaho border.

As they casually moved across cool Grasshopper Creek, White decided to immerse his prospecting pan into the water.

He pulled his battered pan up from the water, swirling the gravel. But this time there was something magically different. This time the gravel reflected a wondrous yellow tint – he had discovered gold. And so, simply put, Montana was born.

As a result of the gold strike, Bannack quickly experienced an explosive growth and became Montana's first territorial capital after Montana was granted territorial status in 1864.

By 1863, six months after Johnston arrived in Bannack, the city had swelled to over 3,000 people in this log and rough-boarded town. Bannack attracted all sorts of people. There was plenty of drinking, gambling and prostitution.

Picture 10
"The Gold Prospectors"
By Frederic Remington

Picture 11
Bannack, Montana Territory, in the 1880's

Entertainment in the town of Bannack included traveling theater groups, dancing parties, sleigh-rides, professional boxing, and an assortment of unsavory "activities."

But Bannack also knew extreme lawlessness. On the south side of Bannack, Skinner's saloon was owned and operated by the infamous sheriff Henry Plummer. Plummer had ridden into Bannack late in 1862, eventually charming himself into being elected sheriff in May of 1863.

But Plummer made weak attempts at keeping law and order by day. But at night, he and his gang of murderers (incredibly calling themselves the *Innocents*) and thieves killed more than 100 people as they ran wild during the dark Montana nights.

Things eventually got so bad that in December of 1863, some miners in nearby Alder Gulch formed Vigilante committees to handle the problem. Within a few weeks, (January 1864) Sheriff Plummer and his gang were hung.

John "Leg-Eating" Johnston?

Did Johnston really eat a Blackfoot warrior's leg? No. Thorpe and Bunker tell us on pages 80 and 81 that Johnston, now a Blackfoot Indian prisoner inside a teepee, was under guard. He chewed through the rope that was binding his hands, overpowered the guard, took his knife, and *"ran the knife's keen edge around the hip and cut to the bone socket."* Then Johnston tears the leg loose from the Indian.

Here is *the truth*. In 1858, a treacherous man named Boone Helm used his knife to remove the legs from a traveling companion who had just committed suicide. It was the middle of winter, and Helm was starving. He ate one leg, and wrapped the other in an old red flannel shirt, tied it across his shoulder, and headed for Salt Lake City.

Interestingly, Boone Helm later joined Henry Plummer's outfit of cutthroats, and was hung, (as was Plummer,) by Beidler and the other vigilantes in January of 1864. The truth is much more fascinating, if not more macabre.

During the vigilante days in Bannack, Johnston associated with his on-again, off-again, friend and partner, John Xavier Beidler. It was Beidler who was Johnston's primary sidekick. "X" Beidler, like Johnston, was a miner who quickly became one of the leaders of the vigilante group in Bannack. The two men apparently had something in common - whiskey and violence.

John Xavier Beidler and Johnston were birds of a feather. Beidler obviously possessed qualities that Johnston admired, and those qualities were perhaps attached to Beidler's callousness, depravity and warped sense of justice and punishment. The following story characterizes Beidler:

"J. 'X' Beidler was a stocky, perpetually drunken man, who cursed both his fellows and God, but played fair with both. When he was a lawman, the newspapers chronicled his activities generally in three terse sentences, in successive issues: 'X' Beidler left yesterday for Bonanza Gulch after horse thieves. Yesterday a man was found hanging in Bonanza Gulch. He is believed to be the horse thief who has been annoying ranchers of the vicinity. Yesterday 'X' Beidler returned to town, after a trip to Bonanza Gulch." (54)

Interestingly, when Beidler recorded his memoirs in 1889, he devoted a half page tribute (some of which is purely fictional) to Johnston.

Incidentally, Johnston and Beidler eventually formed a partnership in Johnston's wood yard in 1868. The men labored as "woodhawks," i.e., cutting wood for Missouri River steamboats. The fearless duo arrogantly conducted their woodcutting business directly under the noses of the Sioux Indians, working in plain sight, on the banks of the Musselshell River. Needless to say, Johnston was always under attack from the angry Sioux.

Picture 12
John "X" Beidler's Gun Set
The Vigilante Committee Presented Beidler With This
Gift Gun Set

Yank or Reb?

Men (and women) from all parts of America, and the world, came to Montana Territory to either look for gold or start a business that would meet the many needs of those self-same gold seekers during the early 1860's. As reported, the particular mining towns to which Johnston rushed in order to "make his fortune" were Bannack, Alder Gulch, and perhaps Virginia City.

If one is to attempt to understand and appreciate the life of Liver Eating Johnston, it is imperative to consider the extreme violence and the political and ideological boiling pot into which Johnston and other Union loyalists were immersed. If one seeks to understand Johnston's motivations leading to his enlistment into the US Army, it is vital to consider the rigors he faced every day in the mining camps.

For example, although Montana Territory belonged to the Union, Montana itself was considered a Confederate enclave. As a matter of fact, Montana's first elected representative to the United States legislature was a secessionist (and ultimately denied a seat in Congress). Liver Eating Johnston clearly recognized the schism into which he temporarily chose to live his life.

With the Civil War raging, one can only imagine how difficult it must have been for Johnston and the other miners as they stood in near proximity to Rebels; Rebels who sought to send gold to their own Confederate States President, Jefferson Davis.

One can most certainly imagine Rebel and Yank exchanging threats and insults, fighting and killing to protect their ideologies in the mining camps.

To compound the problems, there was no organized law enforcement yet established (at least until the Vigilantes were formed – of whom Johnston's friend X. Beidler was chief henchman), so men were free to exact revenge for the hatred they felt toward their new enemies. The tensions, indeed, must have been savage. Much of the west was a legal and jurisdictional nightmare.

Into the Vacuum Flow the Miners

Prior to, and during, the early part of the Civil War, Montana was part of Idaho Territory, and virtually empty of white men. Occasional trappers and hunters dared to venture onto tribal lands in order to make a living. As the war progressed, more and more individuals began to populate mining areas such as Bannack, Alder Gulch and Virginia City.

Many early prospectors migrated to Montana from the South after their terms of enlistment expired in the Confederate Army during the Civil War. Still others escaped to Montana as deserters from battle.

Regardless of the reasons, proof that Southern veterans and sympathizers existed in large numbers was the fact that the Rebels established a mining camp, Confederate Gulch, to honor their three Southern comrades who first discovered gold at the site which would be so-named.

With the Civil War raging (and the sons of the Confederacy and the Union dying in incredible numbers), each side faced an enormous economic drain as they struggled to pay for the cost of their respective wars. When news of the fantastic gold strikes reached Presidents Lincoln and Davis, it became obvious how the newly discovered gold would help fund their wars.

As thousands of Union sympathizers and Rebel secessionists poured into Montana, these hardy, diverse citizens had little desire other than to support their ideologies by attempting to send wagon loads of mined gold back to their respective "countries."

Union supporters knew that the secessionists needed to be displaced from control of the gold mines. Enormous riches in gold had to be stopped from secretly reaching the economically starved Confederate States. Gold would be a he key to Union victory in the Civil War – and indeed it played out that way.

It is important to keep in mind that the gold mines were primarily under the control of Confederate secessionists. After President Lincoln was informed about the untold riches in gold found at Alder Gulch, the United States government immediately recognized the importance of the gold strikes to the war effort.

In all probability, Johnston relished getting into fist-fights with the Rebs. From the research gathered to date, no other behavior would be expected from Johnston. Being as massive as he was, he no doubt struck a mighty picture as he bulled his way from camp to camp, probably in a drunken stupor.

The Importance of Virginia City to the War

As miners, merchants, prostitutes and gamblers filtered into Montana Territory, a town had to be built to accommodate and support their various "needs." The answer was Alder Gulch. The townspeople, mostly southern secessionists, decided to name the town "Varina," thus honoring the wife of their beloved Confederate President Jefferson Davis.

It is fascinating to realize that Varina was essentially a Confederate town resting upon soil that was under the control of the government of the United States. The Civil War was blasting our nation apart – and a group of secessionists decided to plant a town on Union soil, extract Union gold, and plot to transport that Union gold it to Jefferson Davis!

Only the strains of our collective imaginations can fathom what daily occurred at Alder Gulch as the Yanks and Rebs wrested gold from the three or four square miles of the Alder Gulch mining camp.

Although the population around Varina (later to be called Virginia City by Northern sympathizers) was essentially Confederate, some northern sympathizers were quite influential, not only in Alder Gulch and Virginia City, but in Montana Territory itself.

Dedicated Union loyalists like U.S. Army Captain James Fisk (55) brought Northern emigrants and merchants (the first carpetbaggers) from St. Paul, Minnesota, to the Montana gold fields in large numbers, an intentional move "out-populate," and control, the Confederate secessionists and miners.

Another key figure was Sidney Edgerton, a Lincoln supporter and Chief Justice of Idaho Territory. Edgerton planned for the new emigrants to contribute to the Northern war effort in two ways: to either mine the gold or aggressively seek to overpower the Southern secessionists.

Edgerton performed his job so well that he convinced Lincoln to recognize Montana as a territory. He also maneuvered himself into the role of the territory's first governor.

The Rise of Vigilante Justice

The mining towns of Bannack, Alder Gulch and Virginia City, soon grew out of control. Since there was no organized law enforcement in place, the population was free to do as it pleased. Violence became a way of life. Secessionists taunted Northern sympathizers by continually raising their Rebel flag, daring anyone to start trouble. Killing was rampant, and something had to be done.

It was decided by town leaders to secretly meet and form a Vigilance Committee to put down lawlessness and violence. Liver-Eating Johnston's friend, "X" Beidler, gladly volunteered to serve as "strangler" for the group.

The committee's first order was to investigate "troublemakers." Upon completion of the investigation of a purported guilty party, the committee met to decide the alleged criminal's fate. Then they simply, and efficiently, hung the guilty party. Cold, ruthless, and greatly feared, Vigilante terrorism worked so well that quickly there was a noticeable drop in violence and crime.

Because of the growing numbers of Union sympathizers flowing in by wagon train from "back east," Confederate strength began to wane. The Vigilantes made certain that the rebels were continually terrorized, thus preventing the secreting of gold down the Bozeman Trail to the Confederacy.

Picture 13
Vigilante "Justice"

Johnston Leaves Alder Gulch

In May of 1863, a group of miners discovered the extraordinary gold strike at Alder Gulch. It has been reported by several sources that Johnston moved to Alder Gulch from Bannack upon hearing about the phenomenal gold strikes. It now becomes easy to understand how the constant friction between Northern and Southern sympathizers may have been a contributing motivation for Johnston to enlist in the Union Army. He may have become frustrated and angry by what he was exposed to on a daily basis – thus, perhaps, encouraging his decision to enter the war.

Historians have suggested that Johnston decided to leave Alder Gulch only after a few months of unsuccessful placer mining. Authoritative speculation has him departing Montana territory in late 1863 after apparently having no success in striking gold. It was then that he most probably journeyed to St. Louis to enlist.

The problem revolves around the precise period in which Johnston left Alder Gulch. However, it is *possible* that Johnston originally signed with the 3rd Colorado Infantry in St. Louis, Missouri, in February of 1864. The 3rd Infantry was formed earlier in October 1862. Other records exits that also suggest that Johnston initially enlisted with Company A of the 3rd Colorado Infantry.

The precise military unit to which Johnston was first attached deserves comment. The 2nd Colorado Cavalry Company Descriptive Book lists Johnston as initially being placed as a veteran soldier (U.S. Navy) with the 3rd Colorado Cavalry. The problem with this is that the 3rd was actually created in the summer of 1864 with an enlistment period of only 100 days, organized for the express purpose of fighting Indians in Colorado.

The fact is, according to the Company Descriptive Book, Johnston enlisted and enrolled on February 23, 1864 at Benton Barracks, Missouri. He then mustered in with the 2nd Colorado Cavalry on the next day (February 24, 1864), also at Benton Barracks, according to Book "P" Page 202,

Line 26, Sheet 48 of the Transcript of the Records of the Colorado Volunteers in the *War of the Rebellion 1861-1865*. Therefore, there is no way that Johnston could be found in Colorado Territory during the summer of 1864 because he arrived in Missouri five months prior to (at least by February 23, 1864) the formation of the 3rd Colorado Cavalry in Colorado. So, there does indeed seem to be an error in the Company Descriptive Book.

Perhaps the clerk made a simple recording error when he listed Johnston as originally being with the 3rd Colorado Cavalry.

The 3rd Colorado Infantry, stationed in Colorado, eventually marched to Pilot Knob, Missouri in April 1863, where they were assigned guard and clean-up duty until merging with the 2nd Colorado Infantry, thus forming the 2nd Colorado Cavalry, the unit to which Johnston became attached throughout the duration of the Civil War. The actual formation of the 2nd Colorado Cavalry occurred on November 26, 1863, per special order # 278, Headquarters, Department of the Missouri.

Remaining Questions About the Timeline of Johnston

Was Johnston among those 3rd Colorado Infantrymen who made their way to Pilot Knob, Missouri in April, 1863, despite what historians speculate about his departure from Montana Territory after the Alder Gulch strike? Did he remain with the 3rd Colorado Infantry until the unit merged to become the 2nd Colorado Cavalry in November of 1863? If so, then why do his records indicate that he enlisted into the 2nd Colorado Cavalry on February 24, 1864? There is no record of him enlisting in any of the camps in Colorado.

Again, authoritative speculation has Johnston heading directly for St. Louis, Missouri to enlist in the Union Army. He probably was first assigned to the 3rd Colorado Infantry (Company A) until it was absorbed into the 2nd Colorado Cavalry, and then placed in Company H as a "veteran scout."

A Brief History of the 1st, 2nd and 3rd Colorado Cavalry Volunteer Regiments

The Colorado State Archives reported that when President Lincoln called for volunteer soldiers to supplement the regular Union army, almost 5,000 men from the Colorado Territory enlisted. Other Union Army volunteers decided to serve in organized territorial militias assigned to fight Native Americans in Colorado rather than fight against rebel forces.

1st Colorado Cavalry

The composition of Civil War troops from Colorado was unique. Two of its three cavalry regiments were created from pre-existing infantry units. The 1st Regiment of Colorado Infantry Volunteers evolved into the 1st Colorado Cavalry on November 1, 1862 and remained in Colorado until 1865 where it fought against Indians and protected stagecoach routes.

Its most infamous Indian campaign was fought on November 29, 1864 against the Cheyenne at Sand Creek, Colorado. The militia, led by Colonel Chivington, surprised Chief Black Kettle and his band of 500, killing and mutilating over 200 men, women and children, ignoring the fact that Black Kettle's band was under a flag of truce at the time of the massacre.

2nd Colorado Cavalry

According to the 2nd Colorado Cavalry's Company Descriptive Book's footnote, Companies A, B, and E, (2nd Regiment Colorado Infantry) were consolidated with the eight companies of the 3rd Colorado Infantry, which combined to form the 2nd Regiment, Colorado Cavalry in November 26, 1863 in Missouri (the Regiment to which Johnston was finally assigned).

3rd Colorado Cavalry

The 3rd Colorado Regiment of Infantry was originally stationed in Denver and Camp Weld from September 1862 to January 1863. They were attached to the District of Colorado until March 1863. From Colorado, they journeyed first to Fort Leavenworth, Kansas, then to various spots in Missouri (St. Louis, Sulpher Springs, Pilot Knob, Potosi and Ironton).

Finally, they moved back to St. Louis in October 1863, where they consolidated with the 2nd Colorado Infantry to form the unit to which Liver-Eating Johnston was finally attached - the 2nd Colorado Cavalry.

Picture 14 (a)
Civil War Era Cavalry Flag

A
LIVER–EATING JOHNSTON FACTOID

A Candid Portrayal

Liver-Eating Johnston was ...
"an unlearned, unwashed, drunk, and violent... (frontiersman) who tore a bloody swath across the then unconquered American West."

Author Robert Utley

4

The Call of Cannons: The Civil War Years

This chapter presents a comprehensive evaluation of Johnston's Civil War activities. The information on his activities was gathered from primary sources such as government records, period newspapers, military pension records, U.S. Army health records, etc. It provides the reader a fascinating look into the many aspects of Johnston's life as a scout with the 2nd Colorado Cavalry.

Johnston arrived in St. Louis knowing that he signed up for a three-year hitch, fully aware that he would not "muster out" until 1867; sooner, of course, if the war ended prior to his contracted three year enlistment.

Liver-Eating Johnston signed on as "veteran recruit," according to the Record and Pension Office reports of the War Department. His wilderness experiences prior to his enlistment, and his stint in the US Navy, provided him veteran status.

The 2nd Colorado Cavalry was officially placed under the District of Central Missouri, Department of the Missouri, until December 1864. Following re-organization in January 1865, the regiment ultimately mustered out in September 1865, becoming part of the District of the Upper Arkansas.

At war's end, the District of the Upper Arkansas dissolved in September 1865, the same month Johnston mustered out and returned to Montana.

Johnston spent nearly two years serving in the Union Army. He served with both distinction and dishonor, as the reader will soon learn. Johnston was not personally involved in many battles. He apparently spent a lot of time as a Union spy embedded into a Confederate unit. .

Picture 14 (b)
Benton Barracks, St. Louis, Missouri -1860's

No Surprise - Liver-Eating Johnston Deserts

Incredibly, after only five days in the Army, Johnston deserted on leap year day – February 29, 1864, from Benton Barracks. In the Descriptive List of Deserters, Johnston is seen eventually returning to his unit "without being apprehended." Johnston's desertion from the Mexican War and Civil War certainly provides evidence that Johnston's character seemed to drive his behavior.

Although Johnston's brief desertion from Benton Barracks is a matter of record, desertion, in general, during the Civil War, was common. It is worthwhile to examine the degree to which desertion occurred in the Union Army and the general military and civilian attitudes toward it. By doing this, we can develop a better understanding of perhaps why Johnston decided to desert.

In her fascinating book, Ella Lonn, author of "Desertion During the Civil War," stated that during the Civil War, "one hundred thousand Confederates left the ranks while more than two hundred thousand Union soldiers did the same. This amounted to one out of every seven Union soldiers and one out of every nine men in the Confederate Army" (56)

There is no way to uncover the reason or reasons that Johnston decided to desert after only five days in the Army. According to Ella Lonn, there were many motivations that induced a soldier to desert from his unit.

For example, volunteers like Johnston were given a bounty as an incentive to enlist in the US Army. Johnston's signing bonus, according to his unit's Company Descriptive Book, was $300.00; $160.00 paid upon enlistment and the remaining $140.00 to be paid at some later time. Johnston was also paid the grand sum of $13.00 per month in salary.

The bonus, or "bounty" as it was called, was cash in hand. Did Johnston decide to take his bounty, which was equal to a year's salary and simply blow it all in raucous times during his desertion?

Johnston Awaits His Orders

As was mentioned, Johnston did not immediately get into action with the Confederates. His unit remained at Benton Barracks, St. Louis, awaiting orders.

On April 23, 1864, two months after Johnston enlisted, Johnston was re-stationed to Fort Leavenworth, Kansas. At Fort Leavenworth, Johnston was not immediately given any orders. The Company Muster Roll lists Johnston as a 'straggler," awaiting transportation to company." This tells us that Johnston could have been receiving some sort of punishment for his desertion.

His military records contain a notation that mentioned that the "veteran recruit was dropped from aggregate (list of soldiers) by Regimental Order – May 17, 1864 at Sinabar, Mo." (Missouri). Another notation dated May 1864 states that Johnston was an "extra or daily duty cook" during the month of May. However, apparently the reason for this confusion was because he was "not taken up on the aggregate until June 21, 1864, on account of the non-arrival of their descriptive rolls."

There is yet another notation that states "September 1864 – extra or daily duty as Provo Guard." Do all the notations mean that Johnston was on restricted duty as punishment for his desertion? Unfortunately, we will never know. However, during the next month, October, Johnston is finally in battle, suffering gunshot wounds to his shoulder and leg in the battles of Westport and Newtonia, Missouri.

The shoulder wound eventually caused him so much trouble that he applied for, and received, a small pension between the years 1884 to 1900 due to a gradual "withering away," of muscle tissue.

Bushwhackers, Bandits vs. Liver-Eating Johnston and the 2nd Colorado Cavalry

When Johnston first stepped onto Missouri soil in February 1864, the "official" war in that state had been raging since April of 1861, the same month the Confederates shelled Fort Sumter, North Carolina, thus introducing the world to Americas' War of the Rebellion.

The Missouri trouble started when Union troops, under the volatile leadership of Captain Nathaniel Lyon, wantonly killed twenty Southern sympathizers trying to protect the Confederate arsenal near St. Louis' Camp Jackson.

But this action by Captain Lyon was inevitable, the result of an "undeclared" border war between Kansas and Missouri that had taken many lives in the latter 1850's. Kansas, as a territory, was striving to earn statehood, taking advantage of the Kansas-Nebraska Act of 1854 that allowed the territory's residents, by vote, to decide the explosive slave issue.

There were two ideological camps in the territory of Kansas - abolitionists and pro-slavery Southerners. The abolitionists wanted Kansas to be a Free State, thus ending slavery. The Southerners abhorred the idea of Yankee involvement in Kansas. Finally, the slavery issue finally came to a vote – slavery would continue.

The abolitionists became angry over the very loose voting procedures. The pro-slavery group reacted in equal kind, and violence began to fester – a tragic, brutal internal war that was to be defined by the words "bleeding Kansas."

As the violence increased, Federal troops were called to patrol eastern Kansas and Western Missouri; called to protect Union loyalists from the murdering bushwhackers, led by killers William Quantrill and Bloody Bill Anderson.

Hundreds of people were killed on both sides and millions of dollars' worth of real estate and personal property were destroyed during the reign of terror fueled by Quantrill and Bloody Bill.

Liver-Eating Johnston's regiment, the 2nd Colorado Cavalry, fell under the command of Major General James Blunt, Commander of the Department of Kansas. Officially, Liver-Eating Johnston was a scout attached to the 1st Division, 4th Brigade, H Company.

There were 384 men assigned to the unit. Blunt, a Kansan, was considered to be an average-to-below average commander. He was criticized for a lack of imagination, low levels of aggressiveness, as well as for his lack of personal self-discipline. Blunt's was described as:

"...a stubby, overweight man with deep-set dark eyes, a... black moustache, and a pointy goatee. Licentious and coarse, Blunt drank heavily and traveled with a coterie of 'female servants' to tend to his needs. He threw gala banquets, rollicking late-night parties, and grand parades in his honor. He was reputed to be ...thoroughly dissolute." (57)

James G. Blunt was a staunch abolitionist who earned himself a spot in John Brown's underground railroad. He was later handed an Army commission as Brigadier General primarily through the influence of Senator Jim Lane. At the beginnings of the Civil War, Blunt was appointed as a Union commander in Kansas.

Despite his best efforts, Blunt had no success in sealing the Kansas-Missouri border from the guerilla intrusion into Missouri. He apparently had no supporters. One newspaper editor critically wrote the following about Blunt: "this method of protecting burned towns, dead bodies and destroyed private property, don't suit us." (58)

General James G. Blunt was no professional soldier. Prior to his Civil War experience, Blunt was a doctor in Ohio. Then he moved to Anderson County, Kansas, and fell in with the abolitionists. When the Civil War began, he enlisted as a private in the Third Kansas Regiment

Blunt was quickly promoted to lieutenant colonel, serving under General Lane at the Battle of Dry Wood and later took command of a military force that marched into Indian country. Through political maneuvering, Blunt was promoted to brigadier general, commanding troops under the Department of Kansas.

Blunt had received little praise for his leadership abilities. It was obvious that General Blunt's military performance did not attract positive attention from his superiors. As a matter of fact, things began to worsen for Blunt on October 6, 1863. After being put in charge as the Federal Commander of the Indian Territory, Blunt and his men journeyed to Baxter Springs, Kansas, where 400 of Quantrill's raiders attacked Blunt's patrol, killing 103 Union soldiers. Blunt ran away like a frightened schoolgirl.

After this debacle, Blunt was removed from his command due to incompetence. But, through political efforts, Blunt was eventually restored to duty.

The severe attitudes owned by the "bushwhackers," or "Missouri border ruffians," as they were also called, toward Northern sympathizers and Union troops, were clearly articulated by the words of one Southerner: "We will continue to tar and feather, drown, lynch and hang every white-livered abolitionist who dares to pollute our soil." (59)

It was into this cauldron that Blunt and his 2nd Coloradoans became rapidly immersed. General Blunt was hopeful that he would be able to diminish the power of the bushwhackers, but this was not to be. The bloody raids into Kansas continued, frustrating Blunt and tarnishing an already questionable reputation.

Blunt decided to introduce a new strategy in his impotent attempt to stop the bushwhackers – public executions. His goal was to appease the desires of Missourians to see the "heathens" die in front of large crowds of onlookers, as large as three thousand spectators.

By the time Johnston arrived in Missouri, the bushwhacking activities had died down for the winter. Quantrill departed to Texas for the winter, but all of Missouri knew that he and his men would be back in the spring.

<u>A Look at Johnston's Role in the War with the Bushwhackers</u>

It is not precisely known to what degree Johnston got involved in the fighting. We do know, according to a statement on his pension records, Johnston was not present for roll call because he was on detached service as a scout on June 15, 1864.

The 2nd Colorado, under James H. Ford and the Fifteenth Kansas, participated in a hard-fought battle in July of 1864, against Confederate guerillas. When these two units joined ranks to fight, they were called by one journalist as "...the worst body of cut-throats... that ever tortured a victim or looted a community." (60)

Goodrich details a battle scene that typified the style of fighting used by the 2nd Coloradoans. The 2nd Colorado had come up against 140 Confederate guerillas who:

> "...(drew) up in a line of battle, but without halting, the Coloradoans' gave a wild yell, dashed right toward the center of the line which immediately gave way, and after firing a few shots, killing one of the attacking party and wounding another, they fled in wild confusion, with their pursuers (Coloradoans) close in their rear, and seven of them killed before they escaped." (61)

There were several times that the 2nd Colorado was engaged against the Bushwhackers in early 1864, all prior to their involvement with Confederate troops in the territory of Kansas and in Missouri. It all started for the 2nd Colorado Cavalry in April of 1863 when General Ulysses S. Grant needed to withdraw Union soldiers from the Missouri region to help fill the vacuum of Union soldiers who left to fight in Virginia.

The 2nd Colorado was called in from distant Denver in April of 1863 and marched to Missouri where they were to serve as border patrols. It was also decided that loyal Cherokees and African American soldiers were to help fill the vacuum in Indian Territory.

The Bushwhackers knew nothing about the 2nd Colorado Cavalry. The 2nd looked like a rag-tag, undisciplined group of men who would run at the first blast of gunfire or cannon roar. The bushwhackers enjoyed testing the mettle of the Coloradoans. As an example of the Rebel prodding and teasing, the following episode quickly proved to the bush-whacker that the "boys of the 2nd" could hold their own with anyone:

> "In their first skirmish with them (2nd Colorado), Dave Pool, the freebooting (rebel) comedian, dared any of the Colorado 'cowards' to single combat. His challenge was accepted instantly. A Colorado rowdy stepped out between the lines and promptly pinked Dave with a bullet. The Bushwhacker was happy to return alive to his own men. He could grimace and laugh, but his companions knew that they were confronted with formidable fighters." (62)

Chronology of Battles for the 2nd Colorado Cavalry

The following is a list of the battles fought by Johnston's regiment while patrolling areas of Indian Territory and western Missouri. Many campaigns were fought against the Confederate General Sterling "Pap" Price. The asterisks represent the battles in which Johnston participated.

Battles of the 2nd Colorado

1863
Weber's Falls, Indian Territory..........September 9

1864 – Missouri Battles
January 1864 – 2nd Colorado Cavalry ordered to the Missouri border counties of Jackson, Cass and Bates in support of Kansas troops involved with Confederate guerillas.

April 29	Snai Hills
May 21	Snai Hills
May 28	Pleasant Hills
July 5	* Little Blue
July 17	Fredricksburg

October 21	Little Blue	
October 22	Independence	
October 23	.*Westport/Big Blue	(wounded)
October 28	*Newtonia	(wounded)

*=battles within which Johnston participated

Picture 15
War...What is it good for - Absolutely Nothing.

Picture 16
James Butler Hickok (Wild Bill Hickok)
Civil War Union Spy and Scout

Hickok rode into General James Blunt's camp the day
after the Newtonia, Missouri, battle and provided with
an intelligence report of Confederate
General Sterling Price's activities.

In November 1864, General Price had been defeated and the war was essentially over for the 2nd Colorado Cavalry. It was decided that the regiment would be stationed in Fort Leavenworth (Kansas) in December 1864, under the District of the Upper Arkansas.

The 2nd Colorado Cavalry, under newly promoted Brigadier General Ford, was then moved to Fort Riley, Kansas, where they focused their attention on the battles with the Indians. Their primary responsibility was to guard supply trains and wagon trains across Kansas, where the 2nd infrequently fought against bands of Native Americans.

Picture 17
Confederate General Sterling "Pap" Price

Picture 18
Bumbling Union General James Blunt

Some Basic Facts About Johnston's War Record

Johnston Wounded Twice

Liver-Eating Johnston suffered gun shot wounds at Newtonia and Westport. At Newtonia, he was shot in the left shoulder, and at Westport, a bullet dug into his right leg below the knee.

Despite what other researchers have previously stated about Johnston's injuries, none of these wounds were serious enough for Johnston to qualify for a medical discharge. His military records clearly display his presence in camp from January to September 1865, the day Johnston was officially mustered-out of the Army.

Greatly Outnumbered At Newtonia

During the battle of Newtonia, Missouri, Johnston and the 2nd Colorado Cavalry was clearly out-manned by Price's army. In the military records and recollections of General James Blunt, commander of the Army of the Border, Blunt left a powerful written legacy of the valor and courage shown by the 2nd:

Following is an excerpt from Blunts' military letters:

> "In this engagement (Newtonia) the disparity of the number (of the enemy) and the fighting of my command was the most heroic that I ever witnessed. Never (had I seen) such heroism. (It was) unparalleled in the history of the war." (63)

The battle of Newtonia was an immensely crucial battle. General Blunt had Price's army on the run, and a victory at Newtonia would help seal the fate of Price's once powerful command. The 2nd Colorado did, indeed, help to drive Price and his troops into Arkansas.

The 2nd Colorado Runs Out of Ammunition

According to General Blunts' military letters, Johnston's unit was issued 60 rounds of ammunition per man. Once the men exhausted their supply, there was no way to get more unless a dead comrade fell, thereby offering up some hard-gained ammunition.

The 2nd Colorado Volunteers were standing under fire for a long time, without a cartridge to return the deadly fire of the Rebels. The problem was with the Army's supply trains. They were unable to keep up because the rough terrain prevented the wagons from gaining access to the battle line.

A lieutenant named J.B. Pond wrote "that we held our position until our ammunition was exhausted and afterward until succor came, history will tell, and truly; But how, it seems a miracle." (64)

Indeed, that Blunts' army was victorious is a marvelous testament to the quality of soldier who committed his very life, to death if necessary, in order to fight for what he believed in. Blunts' Missouri campaign was so dramatic that he finally garnered commendations for the planning and execution of the Newtonia battle.

The Liver-Eater is Finally Mustered Out

As the Civil War was fizzling out in Missouri, Blunt received orders to begin disbanding some of his troops. Johnston's H Company was demobilized in late 1864 and sent to Fort Leavenworth, Kansas. On November 8, 1864, the Army of the Border was disbanded "by directions of superior authority." The men of Blunts' command had performed their work so well that they were out of a job. And it certainly can be said that no man objected to the demise of Blunts' army.

The 2nd Colorado was no longer fighting the Confederates. Life at the Fort was boring and tedious. Johnston was undoubtedly growing restless awaiting discharge. There is no record to indicate what duties Johnston was involved with while his unit lingered at Fort Leavenworth. Finally, on September 23, 1865, Johnston and the 2nd Colorado were mustered out. The Great War was over.

A Curious Look At Johnston's Military Health Record

Johnston's military health record contains a fascinating section. Included within its contents are details about the dates and illnesses suffered by Johnston during much of his Civil War enlistment:

March 11, 1864	Fever & Ague
March 28 – April 2	Conjunctivitis
May 21 – 29, 1864	Constipation
April 12-30	Conjunctivitis
July 9 – 12, 1864	Constipation
June 1, 1865	Conjunctivitis
December 25, 1864	Conjunctivitis (65)

Johnston's illnesses certainly weren't life threatening, but they were pesky enough to make a soldier feel extremely uncomfortable. Johnston's Civil War wounds would eventually earn him a small pension from 1884-1899.

His wounds, especially the gunshot wound to his left shoulder, would cause him much pain and eventually contributed to his eventual bedridden existence toward the end of his life. Despite Johnston's dubious character, his willingness to join the fight in the Civil War is certainly commendable.

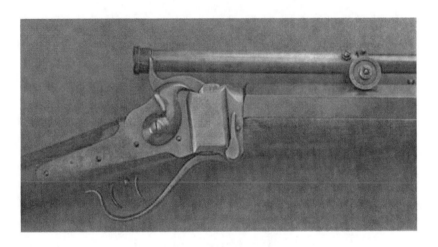

Picture 19
Telescoped Sharps Rifle

Liver-Eating Johnston Owned A Sharps Rifle Similar
To The One In the Above Picture.

A
LIVER-EATING JOHNSTON
FACTOID

<u>Liver-Eating Johnston</u>
Private/Scout
1st Division
2nd Colorado Cavalry Volunteers
4th Brigade
H Company

5

Scraping A Living Under Sitting Bull's Nose

1865-1876

John Johnston returned to Montana Territory unsure about his prospects. What would he do to earn a living? Where would he live? What kind of harrowing experiences would he run into?

We do know that immediately upon his return to his beloved Montana, he was "back in the gold fields both as a prospector and as an Indian fighter."(66) Another newspaper article mentioned that after the Civil War, Johnston,

> "Came to Montana and established a wood camp on the Missouri River near the mouth, where an Indian trading post which was run by (a man named) Clendening and at the time some 16 white men and a few Indians were camped there. The hostile Indians were killing the woodchoppers whenever they could surprise them. The cottonwood trees were cut in cordwood length and piled up in long rows on the riverbanks, and sold to the steamboats going up and down the river. These wood camps were a common sight along the upper Missouri." (67)

Woodhawking was indeed a dangerous business. Only the toughest and most confident men could have handled both the physical and emotional rigors attached to that line of work – especially in the middle of Sioux land. Another interesting account written by Will Carpenter provides an alternate scenario involving Johnston's activities upon arriving in Montana after the war:

"He returned to Fort Benton and obtained a job as a teamster with the Diamond R. freighting company (ranch) out of Fort Benton on the Helena run. He worked at this until the summer of 1867, when he went into a partnership with a man named Sims to cut cordwood for the Missouri River steamboats. The two men established a wood yard just below the mouth of the Musselshell River and spent the winter of 1867-1868 cutting wood." (68)

The Diamond R freighting company was owned by E.G. MacKay and Company. The company held the government contract with the responsibility of freighting goods to Army posts. It was one of the largest freight haulers in Montana Territory. Interestingly, the Diamond R hauled freight for General Gibbon during the Sioux Wars of 1876.

After a falling out with Sim's about his partner's drinking habits, (imagine that!) Johnston elected to get rid of him. In addition, Johnston heard that there were at least three different war parties near the vicinity of his wood yard, so Johnston decided to cool his heels until spring, and took a steamboat back to Fort Benton.

Any break in the action was good news for Johnston. He would usually have a chance to provide townspeople with a spectacle of his drunken excesses. Fort Benton was extremely popular because it was one of the most important early trading posts built at the head of navigation on the Missouri River. Hence, it attracted the best, and the worst, of clientele.

At Fort Benton, Johnston spent what little money he had on drinking. Broke once again, he signed on with the Diamond R freight company, taking supplies to the gold miners at the Forks of the Musselshell. (69)

Johnston Partners With Old Pal J.X. Beidler

Since "X" Beidler was principally a miner, Johnston found Beidler at the gold mine to which he delivered supplies for the Diamond R. This was during late fall of 1868. The two decided to form their own partnership and cut wood back at Johnston's wood yard. It is amazing the ease to which Johnston and Beidler fell into their occupation as woodhawks.

Considering the minute-by-minute danger of attack from the Sioux, the men continued their labors day after day. Perhaps it was Johnston's reputation as "bad medicine" that helped protect he and Beidler.

Liver-Eating Johnston seemed to care little for the notion that the land upon which he constructed his wood camp was Sioux territory. By the very act of his permanent presence, Johnston's actions spoke volumes to the Sioux nation that he would not leave his homestead unless he was "potted" (killed).

Johnston's Self-Imposed Loneliness

The Billings Weekly Gazette (1889) provided the following profile about Johnston as he managed to survive day after day by the sheer brilliance of his woodsman skills:

"Some of the adventures and hairbreadth escapes of this strange individual are, without doubt, among the most wonderful that have ever occurred in the west, and yet, singular to note, they have never yet appeared in print, chiefly perhaps, for the reason that Johnston, though he cannot read (in actuality, he did have the ability to read and write) has superstitions that if his name were to appear in the newspaper, it might perchance, bring him into disrepute among his old acquaintances. The old timers have a particular reverence for Johnston, and whenever his name is mentioned they shrug their shoulders and give up that his record of perilous deeds and thrilling encounters excel those of any other settler in the upper Missouri region. Johnston was one of the very few white men who followed the occupation of hunting and trapping from away back in the '60's, and right in the midst of the Sioux reservation grounds, and while they were the most deadly enemies of his race, he always managed to elude their most crafty efforts at captures. In his fights with the red skins he always came off victorious, and one or more of the copper-colored race was sure to bite the dust through the unerring aim of his rifle. Of course, he was eagerly sought after by the Sioux, and every hour of his existence in those days his life was in jeopardy because of their determined hostility. But like the famed Hannibal, he had the Simon-pure grit, and made an oath to be the mortal enemy of the tribe, an oath which he invariably kept. "(70)

As it was with many frontiersmen, Johnston would build a cabin or some other kind of shelter when he decided to temporarily settle in at a particular location. The isolation of these wilderness abodes made their occupants tempting targets for Indian attacks.

Because Liver-Eating Johnston survived year after year of assaults, the mystique that surrounded him continued to grow, even during his own lifetime.

The Woodhawking Team of Johnston and X. Beidler

It was earlier mentioned that Liver-Eating Johnston and X. Beidler worked together in developing a wood yard that supplied cords of wood for passing steamboats. The early navigators of steamships encountered many problems as they made their way up the rivers of Montana Territory; chief among them was the absolute need to secure a sufficient amount of wood for their steamboats.

Picture 20
John Xavier Beidler in a Younger Man's Clothes

Liver-Eating Johnston and Beidler had to work hard in order to cut enough cords of wood to meet the needs of the large steamers. It took about twenty-five cords of hard wood or thirty cords of cottonwood to fuel the engines of a steamer during a 24-hour period.

Along the lower part of the Missouri River there were plenty of opportunities to supply all demands for wood, for the wood yards were in close proximity to each other. But where the populated communities were more spread out, the steamboat captains had a more difficult time procuring the wood they needed.

Sioux Begin to Supply Cordwood

The Sioux learned that wood was in demand and they used their characteristic methods of trading with the boatmen. They learned that cedar was preferred over cottonwood. So the Sioux would stack up the cedar along the banks where it would be seen by passing steamboats.

The Sioux would also stack cottonwood. The boatmen typically passed up the latter until the Sioux devised the method of smearing the ends facing the river with paint, which made it resemble cedar wood. The thought was that when a steamer stopped, the captain left his vessel to secure wood.

So, the Sioux reasoned that a boatman would rather buy less desired cords of wood rather than go up river with wood in short supply. Another clever means of enticing the boatmen to come for Sioux wood was traced to the change in the channel of the river.

When the water level was shallow so that it would be difficult for the boats to come near shore, the Sioux would walk out for a distance and then sit in the water so only their heads remained above the surface. They wanted to have it appear as if they were standing in the water and that the water was deep enough for the steamers to enter.

One of the chief ways of getting fuel for the boat was in gathering the driftwood, which was piled up on the banks during certain seasons of high water. This was not always satisfactory because it meant very hard work as well as inviting attacks by the Sioux.

Among the hardiest of the western men were those who finally began cutting and collecting wood for the boats and piling it on the shores of the river. These men, like Johnston, Sims and Beidler, were the "wood hawks."

These wood hawks were subject to many dangers in their lives and many of them were killed in their work. The report of the Secretary of War in 1867-1868 showed that seven wood choppers were killed by the Sioux between Fort Benton and the settlements during the summer of 1868.

The work did not appeal to many because of the obvious inherent dangers. The minimum value of the wood was eight dollars a cord. The vocation was thought to be a profitable one for those who succeeded in it. "Wood Hawk Bend" on the Missouri River was the name of an early settlement in tribute to the old woodchoppers and traders.

The Macabre Mr. Johnston

With the increased frequency of steamboats on the Missouri, tourists wanted the opportunity to see what Montana looked like from the safety of the river steamboat.

The tourists were looking for unusual and memorable scenery and landscapes. But on one particular summer day the tourists beheld a sight that would forever be emblazoned on their memories; and, of course, it involved Johnston's wood yard.

In a book entitled "A History of Montana," the author tells of a chilling scene that greeted the tourists as their steamboat paused by Johnston's wood yard. An onlooker named Peter Koch recorded the scene:

"The settlement and surrounding desolate, sage-brush covered plain, did not usually offer many points of interest to the travelers on the steamboats, except the usual features of a village on the extreme frontier, here perhaps somewhat exaggerated; but when the riverboat Huntsville landed there, a sight met her passengers, which was certainly calculated to shock the nerves of any eastern tenderfoot. Along the brink of the river bank on both sides of the land-ing a row of stakes were planted, and each stake carried a white, grinning Indian skull. They were evidently the pride of the inhabitants, and a little to one side, as if guarding them, stood a trapper, well known throughout eastern Montana by the sobriquet of 'Liver-Eating' Johnston. He was leaning on a crutch, with one leg bandaged, and the day being hot his entire dress consisted of a scant, much shrunken, red undershirt, reaching just below his hips. His matted hair and bushy beard fluttered in the breeze, and his giant frame and limbs, so freely exposed to view, formed an impressive and charac-teristic picture." (71)

A differing version of this story is presented below. It details a side of Johnston that was all too common through-out Johnston's life:

"During steamboat days on the Missouri, the Liver-Eater would stand along the river and watch the boats. His costume generally consisted of one shirt, ballooned up by the wind, and a whiskey-soaked, burr-matted beard. When larger boats went by he donned his Sunday clothes – moccasins. He never acknowledged the necessity for trousers except in winter. He gaped at the riverboats and the passengers gaped back, sometimes thumbing their noses, sometimes laughing-to recoil at the hurricane of vituperation launched at them. Their laughter died quickly for another reason. There before them stood thirty white-washed poles in front of Liver-Eaters' place – atop each pole the skull of an Indian bleached to leper whiteness by the dry air of the high plains." (72)

But despite the shocking images that met the travelers' eyes as they gazed upon Johnston's trophies, people stopped to purchase scalps and skulls from Johnston on that day.

Here is a final account:

"The scalps were collected and, together with the heads, were taken to the post. The skulls were boiled until the flesh fell off, then they were placed on a low platform and labeled with various phrases: 'Horace Greeley knows I'm here,' 'On reservation at last,' 'I am for Major Wilkman,' 'I travel for Peck and Darfee.' All the ears were pickled and saved for display and became a great curiosity to the people aboard the steamers coming up river between St. Louis and Fort Benton. Many people bought scalps and occasionally a skull." (73)

This existence seemed to drive Johnston's existence. Johnston was not alone in his macabre human parts business. Mountain men tended to exact the same vengeance on Indian foe as Indians did to whites. It was an expected brutality. It was simply the way of the wilderness.

However, the above referenced demonstrations of savagery were typically Johnston. He seemed to derive great pleasure from shocking people.

A Peek Into the Horrors of Frontier Warfare

In order to appreciate the times in which Johnston lived, and the heinous brutality to which Johnston himself subscribed, following is an actual, but graphic, description of the utter savagery common in the early frontier. The famous Fetterman massacre of 1866 (the battle after which Portugee Phillips made his glorious four day journey to Fort Laramie) provides a horrific account of the brutality participated in by both Indian and white man. A letter by Colonel Carrington attests to his experiences:

> "I was asked to send all the bad news. I gave some of the facts as to my men, whose bodies I found just at dark, resolved to bring all in, viz: mutilations: eyes torn out and laid on rocks; noses cut off, ears cut off, chins cut off; teeth chopped out; joints of fingers; brains taken out and placed on rocks with other members of the body; entrails taken out and exposed; hands cut, sockets, private parts severed and indecently placed on the person..." (74)

The white man similarly exacted this barbaric behavior, especially the mountain men who seemed to relish killing warriors from the Sioux and Blackfoot tribes. The following excerpt is from an early newspaper, which details the tit-for-tat mentality of Johnston and his men during the aftermath of a battle on the Musselshell (Fort Hawley). This is the very battle in which Johnston earned the name "Liver-Eating" Johnston:

"...the boys then quartered (removed arms and legs) the dead Indians and piled them up in one large pile, reserving the heads, scalps and trinkets." (75)

Johnston and Beidler Board the Steamship Nile

The following story is probably familiar to some readers as it appears in virtually all articles written about Johnston. It is given here to establish a timeframe as to Johnston's activities in the late 1860's.

In spring of 1869, the steamship Nile, piloted by the well-known and highly competent Captain Marsh (the same captain who navigated the steamship "Far West" before and after the Custer defeat) picked up Johnston and Beidler, who were entertained while the boat continued it journey.

It so-happened that Captain Marsh was celebrating his birthday on the same day he purchased wood from Johnston. Traveling on the river was easy because it was May, and the Missouri River was swollen due to the melting ice and snow from the past frigid winter.

To celebrate Marsh's birthday, ice cream was prepared for dinner in honor of the event. Ice cream was unknown to Johnston and Beidler, as well as to other wood hawks in the Upper Missouri. The men were shocked that something so cold could be "invented." They viewed the ice cream with suspicion, unable to fathom how anything cold could be created during the heat of May.

Beidler preferred not to admit his ignorance, but Johnston is reported to have started the following conversation: "X, where does this stuff come from?" "Shut up you fool," growled Beidler, bravely swallowing a spoonful of ice cream, "It comes in cans." (76)

Picture 21
John "X" Beidler
This photo was most likely taken during Beidler's
Vigilante Days

Picture 22
Famed Steamboat Captain Grant Marsh.
Marsh invited Johnston and Beidler onboard the steamship
Nile to help celebrate his birthday

Besieged By the Sioux

Johnston's presence on Sioux land caused them to continually attack him in hopes of either killing him or running him off tribal land. Johnston was angry because the Sioux "molested his beaver traps," i.e., stealing his beaver and interfering with his chances of securing pelts and other trophies of a hunter's prosperity.

In those days, to use Johnston's expression, he slept with his eyes "chock open," ready at all times to meet any emergency that might arise. The danger became so extreme that Johnston had to hide himself in swamps and brush much of the time while hunting. While out in the wilderness, Johnston typically ate "meat straight," or raw meat. He had to be equally careful when lighting a fire.

It is said that Johnston kept a strict account of every Indian he killed, but the number grew so large that his friends thought it incredulous that one man could kill so many warriors from within the Sioux and Blackfeet tribes.

Liver-Eating Johnston often devised traps for the Sioux in his attempt to outsmart them at their own game. For example, one day he constructed a large teepee, and after arranging things as if he had made a hasty departure, left some meat poisoned with strychnine inside the tent, which some of the Sioux discovered, and ate. All of the Sioux who ate the meat died a slow, agonizing death.

Johnston had no way of knowing that the warriors who ate the tainted meat were some of the "elite" braves of the Sioux (not that it mattered to Johnston). As a result of their deaths, the Sioux nation practically besieged Johnston for months at his newly built log cabin.

The only way Johnston could obtain food was to slip out at night. If he could not kill game, he ate large quantities of berries and herbs.

One night after returning from one of his evening excursions, he was surprised to discover signs indicating that several Indians occupied his cabin. How many were inside could not be determined. But the crafty Johnston was prepared for all occasions.

As was his practice when building a cabin, he constructed a secret passageway to his cabin, the existence of which only he knew. On this occasion, Johnston crept quietly to investigate the situation.

Through a crevice, he soon ascertained that there were three Sioux, all well armed and waiting for his return. Because he had vowed death upon every Sioux with whom he came into contact, his habit was to shoot a Sioux warrior whenever such an opportunity presented itself

From his secret vantage point, Johnston drew a bead through the crack on the largest Sioux and fired. The brave jumped from the floor and fell dead, shot through the heart. The other two Sioux were so astonished at the noise and sudden death of their comrade that they grabbed their dead friend's body and ran into the woods in fear and confusion.

Liver-Eating Johnston then threw the secret door open and sprang after them, causing them to drop their friend and flee for safety.

Oral tradition has handed down a ridiculous tale about what happened next. This author wonders why Thorpe and Bunker didn't snatch this bit of absurdity for inclusion into Crow Killer. Regardless, the fable states that Johnston ran to the dead Sioux, and dragged him back to the cabin.

Here, tradition tells us, Johnston mutilated the Sioux body "with his teeth" in the most shocking manner, and drank the blood as it flowed trickling from his victim. So much for the outrageous.

Johnston – The Fire Devil

Part of Liver-Eating Johnston's reputation evolved because he was viewed an evil spirit by the various Indian tribes with whom he had come into contact. The Sioux called him *"Fire Devil."* (77)

Johnston earned that name during a Sioux attack when the Sioux showered his wilderness cabin with flaming arrows, thinking that the resulting fire killed their hated enemy. However, always the cunning woodsman, Johnston had escaped certain death by virtue of a previously constructed underground passageway designed to provide egress in anticipation of an attack. The Sioux, Blackfoot, and Cheyenne were quite aware of Johnston; yet, no one was able to kill him.

Liver-Eating Johnston's frontier resume was quite diverse, reflecting an uncanny survival instinct honed for the rigors of life in and among the unforgiving mountains of Montana and Wyoming.

Sioux Vendetta – *Not Crow*

In Thorpe and Bunkers' book, the authors have Johnston on the attack against the Crow. As was proven earlier, the Crow and Johnston were on good terms. But it was the Sioux with whom Johnston had a vendetta.

Johnston regarded the Sioux as hateful enemies. Any chance he had to "pot" one of them, he did so. There is an incident recorded that details a typical fight with attacking Sioux. Johnston and some men were constructing a log bridge to stretch across the Yellowstone River. One day,

"...indians jumped the work party (Johnston's) The cut logs were placed in a square for defense and they were able to hold off the Sioux until night. Knowing the Sioux would not attack again until morning, they sent one of their party across the river to attempt to reach the fort for help, but he was captured. At sun up, when no help came, Johnston thought of a desperate plan. Many of the men were dead or wounded and they were running out of ammunition. Johnston told the survivors to play dead. The Indians moved in to investigate. The leading Indian cautiously came over the top of the barricade, knife in hand. Johnston caught him in mid-air as he dropped toward the ground. Johnston lifted him to the top of the barricade and stuck his knife into his mouth. The gory sight sent the Indians running in the other direction and saved the lives of the remaining men. (78)

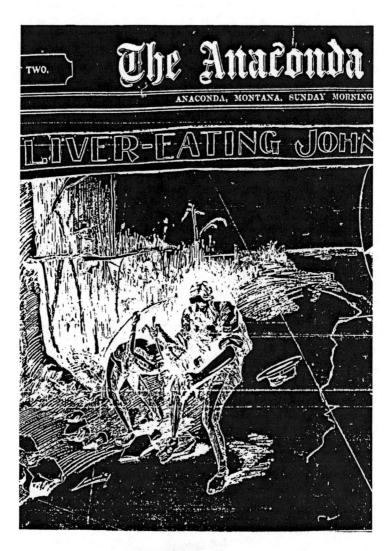

Picture 23
Sioux Combat
This macabre drawing, printed on February 11, 1900, depicts
how the Anaconda Standard Newspaper chose to remember
the lifetime work of Liver-Eating Johnston.

A
LIVER–EATING JOHNSTON
FACTOID

SCALPING 101

After a victim was incapacitated, he/she was typically thrown to the ground, face down. An incision with a knife was made around the hair from the upper part of the forehead to the back of the neck. A foot was placed on the victim's shoulder, and the hair was pulled off with both hands. A distinct "popping" sound was often heard, the result of breaking the suction of scalp to skull. The scalp was then cleaned of blood and fibers.

6

Liver-Eating Johnston Earns His Name

John Johnston never did eat an Indian liver – Crow or Sioux. Yet stories still persist, even in our day, about Johnston's purported eating habits. Since there has been little research conducted about the life of Johnston over the past fifty years since the publishing of Thorpe and Bunkers' Crow Killer, there is still much confusion about the exact manner in which Liver-Eating Johnston earned his name.

There are quite a few different versions of how Johnston secured his peculiar appellation. Many versions have survived, and even evolved, since Johnston's death in 1900. But there is one account that is the most accurate. It takes place at Clendenning's trading post, also called Fort Hawley, at the mouth of the Musselshell. This tiny outpost allowed the trappers and Indians to trade for coffee, sugar, and calicoes in exchange for fine furs and robes.

Reproduced below is a verbatim account, in its entirety, of a story found in the Anaconda Standard (February 11, 1900) that ran a tribute about Johnston two weeks after his death. It is rather lengthy, but yields a most fascinating narrative:

"Liver-Eating Johnston received his particular nom de guerre in an encounter with the Sioux on the Musselshell River near its junction with the Missouri. There were two parties of white men, in all, camped there cutting bull pine and cottonwood for the steamboats. At that time the bloodthirsty Sioux, under the chieftainship of Sitting Bull, were undisputed masters of the vast, trackless plains which stretched far beyond the horizon on both sides of the Missouri. One morning Crow Davis and squaw happened to be the first up in one of the camps. They were a short distance from the camp getting wood for the breakfast fire, when suddenly the squaw told Davis in a low, frightened voice as she continued to pick up wood that Indians surrounded the camp. Crow Davis was shrewd enough to show no signs of his knowledge of the danger, and after picking up a few more sticks of wood walked slowly and unconcernedly back to camp as if nothing had happened out of the ordinary. The squaw kept on gathering wood to keep up the bluff, all the time her cunning black eyes searching the surrounding woods for signs of Indians as she slowly worked herself back to the camp. But the strain was too much even for her stoical nature and finally, a moment after Crow Davis reached the camp, she gave a frightened scream, dropped her armful of wood and ran for the cabin. She never reached it. When about half way to the cabin, a bullet from an Indian's gun found her and stretched her on the ground, a victim of too much courage or too little fear. The wound was not fatal, however, and she lived for many years afterward. In the meantime, the camp had been alarmed by Davis and the shot brought them all to their ready for business. It did not take long to get the sleep out of a man's eyes in those days. Like a flash they dropped behind nearby trees and stumps, ready for the attack. The Indians started off in a mad gallop toward the distant hills. A moment more and they were lost to sight in a rolling depression in the prairie. But they were soon seen climbing the rise of the other side in the far distance. It was a clever trick, but it did not for a moment fool an old Indian fighter like Johnston. While a small party of Sioux had ridden toward the hills, trusting to the distance to confuse their movements, the larger part of the Sioux had made a detour and returned to a deep coulee, which opened, into the Musselshell bottom. Pomp Dennis offered to reconnoiter while the rest of the whites kept up their bluff of not knowing the Sioux was near. Dennis had with him in camp two Newfoundland pups. They were untrained and followed him as he craftily crawled to the top of the small hill which commanded a view of the coulee. Dennis had hardly had a chance to size up the contents of the which he found full of redskins, before one of the pups ran up to the edge and looked over. In a second there was a whir and the dog fell to the ground pierced with a dozen arrows which quivered in his body and a dozen others fell around him. The other dog ran up to its mate and in an instant met a similar fate. The arrows had been falling too close to Pomp Dennis for comfort – it was a miracle he was not hit – and having got all the information he was after, he crawled back the way he had come and reported the result of his investigation. Johnston then developed his plan of campaign. Three men with Winchesters were sent across the river to take up a protected position which commanded the coulee, while Johnston divided the rest up so that no avenue of escape from the coulee was left open. After the men were all placed, the music began, and it was very lively. It was a complete surprise to the Sioux who were picked off like rats in a trap by the men across the river and when a redskin would stick his warlock above the bank of the coulee he at once became good and virtuous. The men across the river did not waste a shot. An Indian fell at every shot and when after a while they found that escape was hopeless that they were simply being slaughtered, they began to dig holes in the bank as protection against the murderous fire. But it availed them but little. The men on the riverbank would change positions a little and find them out. Seeing the hopelessness of the struggle, the Indians demanded a pow wow. Johnston answered them. They told him that they had got all the fighting they could stomach; that they wanted to quit and call the affair a draw. But Johnston would make no terms. The Sioux must be treated to a dose of their own medicine. "If you want to go," he said, "you know the road and there is nothing to hinder you from hitting it." As he said this, an Indian who had crept and crawled beyond the lines made a dash for life. An instant later he sprang into the air and fell with a bullet through him. There was no more pow wowing after that and the Indians understood that their own merciless cruelty was being meted out to them in the order of "no quarter." For some time afterwards the whites kept potting the Sioux in the coulee, while the Indians were unable to do any damage at all with their arrows and guns they possessed. Finally, they concluded to take the desperate chance of a rush in a bunch from their trap. They crept up to the edge of the bank and then, yelling like demons and running like antelope, made a break for the open prairie and life. But they had simply run into another trap. Their maneuver in the coulee had been observed, and Johnston, guessing what they were planning to do, had posted most of his men in a little hollow toward which the Indians, their ranks frightfully thinned, were heading. The men across the river kept raking the running Indians with a deadly fire of which every shot rendered a good account of itself. And then, when in close range, and not a hundred feet from the hollow, they ran into such a merciless hail of lead that they were mowed down like grain. One volley and the fight was over and 60 dead Sioux were stretched lifeless on the plains, a good day's work for a little band of 15 pioneers. But the affair was not yet completed. Quite a number of wounded had crawled off to hide in the bottoms along the river. It was decided to let not a single one escape, as it would mean certain death for some one of the white party. Several Indians were found. Some begged piteously for life and received the finishing stroke with the traditional stoicism. Some begged piteously for life and received the finishing stroke with the traditional stoicism of their race. Johnston found one buck as he was crawling away toward the prairie seriously but not fatally wounded. He trailed him for some distance by the blood splashed on the ground and grass, and as the Sioux warrior heard Johnston he turned to make a last desperate fight for life. Crawling behind the sagebrush, he waited until Johnston was close upon him and let fly his arrow on its errand of death. But the Indian was well nigh exhausted by the loss of blood and the shaft was poorly aimed. It whissed dangerously, but harmlessly, by Johnston's head. Johnston was upon him in an instant, but the Indian was now unarmed and defenseless. Johnston dropped his rifle and pulled out his hunting knife and felt the edge on his nail. "I'm goin' to kill you," Johnston said to the Indian, for he spoke Sioux like a native. "I'm going to scalp you first and then cut your throat like a dog's." The Indian looked at him with cynical indifference and met his fate like a stoic. Grabbing the scalp lock, Johnston pulled it tight with his knee against the Indian. With the other hand he gave a quick slash with his knife around the base and then a sharp pull and the trophy of Indian valor came off with a report like a small pistol - frightful agony as it must have been, yet not a moan or a word escaped the Indian's lips, but two great tears rolled down the doomed Indian's face. Seizing the Sioux by the big brass rings which he wore in his ears, with a quick movement Johnston threw the Indian over his bent knee, and twisted his head around until every cord and muscle of the neck was tense and taut, gave it one quick, ugly sweep of the knife and the painted head came off in his hand, dripping a crimson flood, while the blood spurted in gushes from the headless trunk, which slipped to the ground. He walked quickly back to his comrades, his rifle in one hand and his bloody knife in the other. When he reached the group, one of them, a pilgrim, noticed a little piece of flesh hanging on the knife's blade, and inquired what it was. "That," said Johnston, glancing at the knife, "is a piece of the Injun's liver. I just had a feast off of one and thought maybe some of you *would like a taste—try it!*" (italics mine). And he passed the knife with the little piece of flesh around the circle, none of the men appeared to be hungry for that particular cut. With apparent offense at having his tid-bit slighted, he said, "You don't know how good it is. I eat nothing else when I'm out on the plains if I can get Indian livers. They taste best raw." With that he lifted the knife to his mouth, made a motion as if he was eating the stuff. In reality he had dropped it to the ground by a twist of the hand, but the broad red splatch across his black heard gave the spectators a contrary opinion. From that day on, he was known far and wide as "Liver-eating Johnston. (79)

The Billings Times Newspaper Account

The following is a record of Liver-Eating Johnston's own personal account of his participation in the Cheyenne/Sioux wars as told to a reporter:

"As chief of scouts," said Liver-Eating Johnson, "I was ordered with a dozen other men, you know most of them, and you know also that among his scouts General Miles always had a pet. Well, it was early morning when we started out to look for Indians and in crossing a creek the ice broke and I got wet. After I got dry, I looked down the river and I saw a bunch of squaws coming and we waited and took them all in. General Miles came up and wanted us to go and see what the Indians wanted and I told him they wanted scalps and that he would find a thousand of them. So he told his pet, Yellowstone Kelly, to go and bring them in. Of course, we scouts went too and under a hill we saw plenty of Indians, and we struck back to timber and to hold a cliff for protection. The balls came thick and fast but we held our ground until dark, when we jumped our horses off the cliff and beat it back to where General Miles was camped." Johnston told me that the Indians reported about 40 killed and as many horses, and the next day the Cheyennes came and would have wiped out Miles off the earth, "if it had not been for me. I discovered them coming and Miles got his train in motion and hit the back trail. It snowed and rained and the Indians pulled out." That was Liver-Eating Johnston's story of how 10 scouts held off 1,000 Indians for hours..."(80)

The Virginia City Madisonian News

Liver-Eating Johnston's obituary appeared in the Madisonian News shortly after his death in January, 1900:

"After the Civil War, 1865 found him (Johnson) back in Montana and from that time until the capture of Sitting Bull he camped on the trail of hostile Indians and saved the lives of many early-day settlers. He served as chief of scouts for General Miles in 1877 and participated in more raids against the red-skins than any other Indian fighter in the west.

It is related of him that he took more scalps in those eventful days than anybody." (81)

The Dillon Examiner

Another version of the above referenced article was printed in the Dillon Examiner. Although similar in most respects, there are some additional experiences included that provide interesting reading.

"Johnston was attached to General Miles' command immediately after the Custer massacre. Miles sent him and ten men out to locate the Indians. Johnston told me that he and his men found the Indians in force behind a hill. The scouts retreated to a hill...for natural protection. The Indians made their attack. The white men were well armed and under cover, and while the Indians made a vicious attempt to dislodge them, were kept away by telling fire of the scouts. During the course of the day's fighting more than 40 Indians were killed while Johnson's men escaped without a single casualty. When night came the Indians retired, and the scouts under cover of darkness managed to elude the Indians and get back to General Miles' camp. Johnson advised Miles to withdraw his forces, and Miles took the advice. He broke camp and marched away with his little force. The next day a strong detachment of Cheyenne joined the big force that had been stood off so successfully by the Liver Eater and his men. The Indians prepared to give battle. But by the time the Indians reached the place where the soldiers had camped, Miles and his men were far away. Men...claimed that the Liver-Eater saved the life of General Miles and his small force, by the gallant fight that they put up against the Indians and the timely advice they were able to give Miles." (82)

The Post

On December 24, 1884, an article appeared in the Pioneer Press of St. Paul, Minnesota, written by an unnamed officer of the 7th Cavalry under whom Johnston served during the Nez Perce War. This officer made some negative comments about Johnston's role as scout for General Miles. The letter greatly angered and offended Liver-Eating Johnston. So he decided to refute the unnamed officer's chide, by writing and publishing an article in the Post, which was published on December 25, 1884. Despite what some researchers think, Johnston could read and write, as was noted in his military records.

Johnston's letter was undoubtedly "ghosted" by another person because the letter's contents include sophisticated concepts and vocabulary. Following are the two letters in question. The first letter belongs to the unnamed office with who Johnston was angry. The second letter is Johnston's response to the affront delivered by the officer.

Officer's Letter

"The first time I ever met Liver-Eating Johnston, the scout, said the officer of the Seventh horse, was in '77, when we were out after the Nez Perce. It was a pretty lively campaign that summer, and what with Howard, Miles and Sturgis in the field, all trying to capture Chief Joseph, good scouts were in demand; for every small party detached from either of the three columns operating against the Indians must have a guide; and he must be one who knew his business, able to detect the faintest signs of Indians, and quick and sure on the trail. Johnston came to use from the Crow Agency at Stillwater, where he spent most of his time. He was what is called a 'squaw man,' that is, one who has one or more squaws to wife, and who practically lives with the Indians. A tall, burly fellow, standing over six feet in his moccasins and weighing over two hundred pounds, his strong, well-knit muscular form and his face, framed in an amplitude of flowing beard and curly locks, would have made him conspicuous in a crowd anywhere. He was a first-rate scout, bold and quick to scent danger. But with all his keenness while scouting, I noticed Johnston took mighty few chances himself, and ran no risks that could be avoided. Coming across some very fresh signs of bear while hunting, I asked him to go in the brake with me and see if we could find the game. With a perfectly sober face, he said, 'Well, lieutenant, you and your man go in and stir him up, and I'll shoot him when he comes out the other side.' One day while scouting near the mouth of the Musselshell, he pointed to a belt of timber near at hand and remarked 'there is where I got the name of Liver-Eating Johnston. You see, there was a party of twenty of us hunters and trappers camped here in 1868. The country was full of game and Indians, and beaver was almost as thick as buffalo. We was having splendid luck, and our camp was just piled with peltry. But one morning we was jumped by a band of about fifty Sioux, who circled towards us, whooping and yelling like devils, and firing under the necks of their ponies. We gave them a volley, and the Indians, thinking we were armed with the common rifle, rushed in. But most of us had repeating rifles (it was the first season we had them in the territory), and as they came on we gave them another round which fairly staggered them, but when we pulled on them again, a more surprised lot of bucks you never saw. They skinned out quick, but we gave it to them. I saw one buck tumble from his pony and crawl into the brush, so I went after him. Putting my knife into him I gave it a turn, and when I pulled it out there was a piece of his liver sticking to the knife. So I held it up and yelled to the fellow next to me, 'Say Jim, won't you have a bite? That's all there is to the story. Some say I ate it, but it's a lie.' They do say that Johnson really ate a piece of the liver as Indians sometimes do, believing they acquire the brave qualities of the man they had killed. I remember one day while scouting with a detachment we came upon Chief Joseph's trail. It was near the foot of the Heart Mountain, and miles away from the column of Sturgis. The trail was very fresh and at a little distance ahead of us could be seen the bodies of two white men. As soon as Liver-Eating, who was in the lead, struck the trail, and saw the bodies lying there, he came galloping back, and yelled out, 'there will be more than a million Indians here inside ten minutes.' Well sir, you could have knocked me down with a feather, for I was scared; and when I looked around, and saw the white faces of my men, more than half of who were green recruits, I was afraid of a stampede. But I instantly gave the word to dismount, leaving every fourth man to hold the horses of the others. This, of course, prevented the men from stampeding; and then I ordered the scout to ascend the hill in front and look for Indians. He refused at first, but I told him he was a dead man if he disobeyed. Having seen I meant business, (and I would have shot him sure), he rode on. Cautiously, he ascended the hill but found no Indians."

The reader can clearly observe why Liver-Eating Johnston reeled at the contents of the article. In response to this affront, Johnston submitted the following response to the Post, which was published on Christmas Day, 1884.

Johnston's Response

"In the Pioneer Press of the 21st instant (21st day of December), nearly a column is devoted to a sketch about myself and some of my adventures as detailed to the credulous reporter of that paper by a Jim Crow subaltern of the 7th Cavalry. The smart aleck who undertakes to tell the Pioneer Press about me has not the manhood to back up his statements by publishing his name. However, I suspect who he is and am inclined to think him as big a poltroon now as he showed himself to be when a petty lieutenant in the Nez Perce war. He says that when I was guiding the 7th through the mountain region, I showed the white feather when I struck the Nez Perces fresh trail. Now, the less a good many of the officers of the 7th have to say about the Nez Perces war the better, for their reputation for valor. Some of these days I shall publish what I know about the march of the Nez Perces from Bald Ridge to Bears Paw, and I can promise my friend the fresh lieutenant who is so anxious to tell the Pioneer Press his adventures that I shall add some reminiscences of great interest to himself and some other of his brother officers who I know to be much braver in attacking a beefsteak than a hostile camp. When the 7th was in the region of Clarke's Fork Canyon, I discovered the Nez Perces on Bald Ridge. I told the lieutenant in charge of the detachment that I had found the Indians we were looking for. He looked through his field glasses but said he could not see them. He didn't want to. He hadn't lost any hostile Indians, I guess. The Crow scouts present at this time also saw the Nez Perces and told this brave officer so, but he wasn't open to conviction. None so blind as those who won't see. When the Nez Perces were discovered at Clarke's Fork Canyon, General Sturgis asked my opinion as to the best route to overtake them. I advised him strongly to remain just where we were, as from the lay of the country the Nez Perces must pass close to our encampment that they could then be attacked to advantage, and the campaign ended. General Sturgis saw the truth of my reasoning and agreed with me, as did Captain French and Colonel Benteen. All the other officers of the command demurred and overruled these three officers. They did so because they were afraid to fight, and I told them so at the time in the presence of the command. This bluntness on my part offended some of these sucking warriors, and one of them, the Pioneer Press's informant, has undoubtedly never forgiven me. The result of the council was that we moved on towards Stinking Water, and the Nez Perces passed by our rear and went on their march to Bear Paw, thanks to the blundering and cowardice of these carpet knights. During the balance of the campaign, I was leading scout and guide for Sturgis's command, and part of the time for Howard's and at times for both together. Both these officers during the campaign and after its close gave me the highest praise for my knowledge of the country, skill in guiding troops and intrepidity in a hostile country. I deny that I am or ever was a squaw man or ever kept a squaw as a wife or otherwise. Any statement to the contrary is a malicious falsehood. As far as "sand" goes, I don't need to go to any second-class lieutenant for it. I have been in forty different Indian fights, and have fought them from California to the Gulf of Mexico. I have killed more Indians than all the officers of the 7th Cavalry put together, throwing the regiment in. If the dirty, cowardly officer of the 7th Cavalry who has tried to stab my reputation, through the Pioneer Press, will publish his name, the first time I strike his trail I'll make him think that a section of the Day of Judgment has struck him. My adventures and my conduct are pretty well known throughout the west, and I don't need to go away from home to get a certificate of good character, but it does rile me when a whelp of an officer that was nearly scared to death in one little campaign, comes barking and snarling at my heels, who can count twice as many coups as he can toes and fingers." (83)

Both letters are quite interesting. But the strength of Johnston's vigorous defensive stance to the officer's comments smacks of the famous Shakespearean line, *"Me thinks thou dost protest too much."* It's no surprise that Johnston was criticized by the Lieutenant. But ultimately, we will never know the truth, but it is clear that not a few of his military superiors commended him for his scouting skills.

The Daily Leader – False Report of Johnston's Death

In another fascinating article published in 1878, a false report had been circulated that Johnston was killed in Montana. The focus of the article is General Sturgis' reaction to Johnston's purported "death." The article certainly corroborates what Johnston had to say in his response to the Post about his duties as scout with Sturgis.

On Friday, January 25, 1878, the Daily Leader of Wyoming reported that Johnston had met a violent death by Indians "on the Yellowstone." The erroneous announcement was first recorded in the St. Louis Globe Democrat and then spread to other newspapers throughout the west.

Following are the full contents of the 1878 article featuring and interview with General Samuel Sturgis, for whom Liver-Eating Johnston served as scout while pursuing Nez Perce leader, Chief Joseph.

For ease of reading, both General Sturgis' and the reporter's comments are clearly delineated below:

"The announcement of the death of 'Liver-Eating' Johnson on the Yellowstone caused the St. Louis Globe boy to interview General (Samuel) Sturgis, whose guide he was during the pursuit of (Chief) Joseph. He said…

<u>INTERVIEW</u>

Sturgis:

"I met him when we were at the mouth of the Stillwater, and there engaged him as a scout on account of his knowledge of the country which we were to go over last summer."

Reporter:

"What do you know of his Indian fighting, General?"

Sturgis:

"Personally, I know nothing; though, from all I heard, he had killed quite number of Indians, by whom he was greatly feared."

Reporter:

"That's a rather peculiar *nom de' guerre* he travels under (Liver-Eating), General."

Sturgis:

"Well, yes," laughing, "that's the name he was known by, though, universally – 'Liver-eating' Johnson – and I have no doubt earned it honestly. He was, as you may readily suppose, quite a character. I never heard the full particulars of his liver-eating exploit;

but I have the best reason in the world for believing its truth – he told me himself."

Reporter:

"He possessed the accomplishment of truth, then, among others?"

Sturgis:

"He was a perfectly truthful man. In all my dealings with him I never knew him to deviate a line from the truth. He never professed knowledge which he did not possess.

Reporter:

"What sort of a looking man was he, General?"

Sturgis

"Looked like a quiet going farmer. He was a man of fifty-one years of age, stoutly and powerfully built, with a sober, resolute face, dark hair and eyes, and heavy black beard."

Reporter:

"Quite picturesque, then?"

Sturgis:

"No, he wasn't at all picturesque. He might have been if he chose, but these guides, as a rule, make no attempt at personal adornment, and Johnson in particular, was utterly regardless of his clothes. He was very carelessly dressed at all times, consequently it was impossible to guess at his merits from his personal appearance. Well... well... I'm sorry he's dead but (looking at the death notice again) it doesn't say how he came to be killed. Have you heard any further particulars?"

Reporter:

"Nothing further than what you see there. Maybe he has been killed in a fight probably"?

Sturgis:

"I hardly think so. Very few people in the country would care to engage him, and he never sought trouble. On the other hand, he always avoided personal encounters, though when he was forced into one he could take care of himself admirably. No... I don't think he has fallen in a fight. I see by the report that the impression may arise that he killed Indians while he was with me. He was not present at the fight."

Reporter:

"How did that happen, General?"

Sturgis:

"The day before I caught the Indians I sent him off from the mouth of Rocky Creek, on Clark's Rock of the Yellowstone, toward Crow Agency, to intercept the supply trains and bring them up."

Reporter:

"I suppose there were occasions when he was invaluable to you?"

Sturgis:

"Yes, indeed, and never more so then when I crossed the river in order to go to Miles' relief, fearing that Sitting Bull might come to the rescue of the captured Indians. I heard he had intercepted the Nez Perce, so I crossed the river with the whole command to the scene of the fight. Johnson was my guide on that occasion. Everything depended upon him – no one else in the command knew anything about the country we had to traverse – and he led us straight to our destination."

Reporter:

"What sort of man was he basically?

Sturgis:

"These men are pretty much alike. They live from hand to mouth, make a little money and spend it as soon as is made; live principally by the chase and seem to have no care for the future."

Reporter:

"Married or single?"

Sturgis:

"Oh, I've no doubt that he was, or had been, married. The marriage relation is not very seriously regarded in that country. Such men marry squaws generally according to the Indian custom, but the relation is not considered very binding, and Johnson may have been married more than once…" (84)

The Close of Johnston's Indian Fighting

The end of the Sioux, Cheyenne and Nez Perce wars effectively brought to a close the Indian fighting career of Liver-Eating Johnston. Johnston was now fifty-three years of age, still unsettled, with no prospects. Except for the gold strike at the Judith River, the gold fields had essentially been played out. The only way that Johnston could make a living was by hunting and trapping, whiskey peddling and occasional guiding.

A Wife for Liver Eating Johnston?

After the campaign with the Nez Perce was concluded in 1877, an interesting meeting occurred between Sergeant Jacob Horner, who marched west with Custer, and a Crow woman who told Horner she was the wife of Johnston:

> "During the march (to Fort Rice), the regiment (7th Cavalry), was encamped one day near an Indian agency at which a number of Crows also were in camp. With two companions, Horner wandered over to inspect them. Seeing several squaws seated on the ground, one of the cavalry-men remarked to Horner, 'How would you like to have a squaw?' To the astonishment of the three soldiers, she turned about and with flashing eyes berated them soundly in good English. She told them, Horner said, 'that she was the wife of "Liver-Eating" Johnson, well known frontier character, who participated in the Nez Perce campaign in a civilian capacity." (85)

Scouting in 1878

We know that Johnston was still involved in scouting in 1878 because of an incident related by fellow scout and buffalo hunter, Vic Smith. Smith recorded that a friend of Liver-Eating Johnston's name George Johnson "one of nature's noblemen, drowned in the Musselshell River in '78 while scouting with Jack (Johnston)..."(86) There is no indication for who Johnston was scouting or the purpose for which he was hired.

Johnston Arrives At the Hoskin/McGirl Trading Post

In the spring of 1879, Johnston is found at the Hoskin and McGirl stagecoach and trading post, which was located where the Montana town of Huntley now stands. The trading post was described as:

"(A trading post which) was doing a thriving business. It was a horse market, a chamber of commerce, a social center, the Mecca toward which trails of all plainsmen eventually led. Prospectors from the hills came in to toss down little sacks of gold dust in exchange for bacon and coffee and flour and sugar so they could go out into the hills again. Merchants from the East brought in beads and calico and whiskey. Trappers brought in their furs and hides. Indians came with horses to exchange for other horses, and with buffalo and elk hides to exchange for coffee and calico and beads and sugar - much sugar." (87)

Johnston was at this trading post exchanging pelts and hides. Beaver fur during the summer months was not worth the taking because the beaver shed its thick fur; hence, it's poor quality. Hunting beaver during the frigid winter was not a practice because the beaver lived safe and secure in its home of frozen mud and tree limbs and twigs.

Trappers like Johnston would compress eighty beaver pelts to make a standard "pack" which was then secured tightly with buckskin thongs in preparation for the sale.

There wasn't much of a remaining market for beaver pelts as compared to the early years of the 1800's. But there was obviously enough for trappers to bring their beaver "plews" into the trading post to exchange for cash or goods.

Johnston brought in wolf skins. As a wolfer, it was customary to pour a poison called strychnine on the flesh of a dead buffalo or antelope. When the wolves feasted upon the dead beast, death would quickly occur. It would not be unusual to kill an average of sixty wolves per day. In 1879, wolf hides were worth $3.50, while buffalo hides sold for a mere $3.00. Vic Smith reported that he once earned $617.00 for one week's worth of wolfing. The buffalo-hunting season extended from late-fall to early spring. Simultaneously, many buffalo hunters also slaughtered wolves, selling the hides to the highest bidder.

No Love Lost On Wolfers

The manner in which wolfers, like Liver-Eating Johnston and Vic Smith, obtained wolf hide disgusted most people. Helen Sanders, in her important work "A History of Montana," wrote about the disdain people had for men who made their living by poisoning wolves. For most hunters, poisoning wolves provided the easiest means of earning an income. Since wolves were considered a nuisance, and occasionally dangerous, hunters felt little remorse for their deeds. Sanders describes the methods by which wolves were killed:

> "About the same time (the end of the buffalo herds in the early 1880's) came the reckless, renegade horde called 'wolfers,' who were, generally speaking, composed of the 'scum of the earth.' Their particular traffic was in wolf-pelts. Poisoned meat was set for a wolf and the animal thus killed, left for bait (usually a buffalo). The cannibal-pack descending upon the meat, perished, and the pelts were easily obtained. These pelts were light of weight, easy to transport and commanded good prices. The vagabond "wolfers," like the worst type of early trappers, and later "hide-hunters," caroused, led licentious lives, and created trouble with the Indians." (88)

It was no surprise that Johnston chose to make a living in this manner. Many men found wolfing to be a very easy way to earn ready cash. With a wolf-pelt selling for $3.50 in the early 1880's, Johnston probably made a considerable amount of money by killing wolves in this manner.

A Close Call with the Crow at Hoskin's & McGirl's Post

Johnston was in the company of some fellow trappers while at the Hoskin and McGirl trading post, among them "Uncle" Billy Hamilton, Hi Stewart, and Doc Allen. Several

Crow Indians were also at the trading post. One Crow had Hamilton's stolen horse, which bore his brand.

After confronting the Crow Indian, the Indian refused to give up Hamilton's horse, stating that he had purchased it legally. It appeared as if Hamilton and the Crow were going to fight. Other Crow flowed over to where the argument was ensuing, as did Liver-Eating Johnston and the other trappers – all parties at the ready to defend their comrades. All hands were firmly placed on their weapons, ready for use in an instant. But suddenly, into the trading post rode Hamilton's Crow friend, Plenty Coups

The young warrior, Plenty Coups, forced the young Crow brave return the horse to Hamilton after Hamilton provided written proof that the horse was his. Angry, the young warrior walked away, brooding, but alive.

Johnston Enters a Tobacco "Spitting" Contest at the Hoskin & McGirl Trading Post

Another unusual incident involving Liver-Eating Johnston also occurred at the Hoskin & McGirl trading post. Johnston's friend, "Uncle" Billy Hamilton, was known far and wide as Montana's best "spitter."

It was decided that Hamilton needed to be challenged and knocked out of his vaunted position as "champeen' tobacee' spitter." The following narrative provides a humorous description of the "contest" in which fifty-four old Johnston participated:

"Liver-Eating Johnson, Bill Hamilton, Tom McGirl and Doc Bill Allen were standing in a row, boots squarely against a straight line drawn in the dust. On each young weather-beaten face was the same strained do-or-die expression. Johnson spit first; his introductory shot hit the little white stone set up as a target twelve feet away, but his second merely spattered the dust near it, while the third went wild. Bill Allen did no better, and no one was surprised. Neither of these men claimed to be prize spitters. McGirl chewed long and vigorously, fixed a determined eye upon the target, and spit. The first time he missed by a good six inches. The second shot, however, and also the third, hit the stone. Two out of three – that was pretty good for McGirl, but probably not good enough, for Uncle Bill Hamilton was coming up, and any man competing against Uncle Bill in a spitting contest was simply handing out donations, bidding "goodbye" to his dollars before he began. Bill prepared himself for the ordeal. He jerked up his buckskin pants and pushed his fur cap far back on his shaggy head. He chewed and spit – and hit a cactus four inches from the stone. Hamilton gave vent to a sound and his blood boiled. He took his time, chewed, glared at the little white stone, puckered up his mouth, and tried again. Again he missed, and the third time he missed. Gloomily in a silence that spoke eloquently of his mortification, he pulled a dollar from his pocket and tossed it to McGirl..." (89)

Incidentally, Billy Hamilton was probably the old west's most competent Indian sign talker, i.e., using the hands to communicate with various tribes. Fellow frontiersmen were typically awed by the skill with which Hamilton developed as his reputation grew over the years.

Picture 24
Fellow "Spitter" Tom McGirl

Picture 25
"Uncle" Billy Hamilton
Hamilton was considered the best Indian
"sign talker" the West ever produced.

A
LIVER–EATING JOHNSTON

FACTOID

POMP DENNIS

Pomp Dennis, one of the characters mentioned earlier in the Anaconda Standard newspaper story, was one of the woodsmen with Johnston on the day that Johnston "earned" the name 'Liver-Eating' Johnston. Dennis was a Confederate soldier captured during the Civil War and "banished" to the upper Missouri River. Dennis came from Fort Benton in 1864 and made a significant gold strike at Confederate Gulch.

7

The Fort Benton Whiskey Peddler

1868-1873

John Johnston and X. Beidler apparently gave up wood hawking shortly after the battle with the Sioux; the battle wherein Johnston earned the name "Liver-Eater." Still in his prime at forty-four, Johnston began to search for other ways to earn an income.

Although still active in securing the pelts of beavers, wolves, bear and buffalo, Johnston looked for more, especially in the "off season" when pelts and skins were of poor quality. Realizing that there was money to be made by supplying whiskey to anyone who could pay for it, Johnston began selling bootlegged whiskey from about 1869 -1873.

With his home base at Fort Benton, he soon had lots of customers. Hundreds of white men made Fort Benton their headquarters. They would organize themselves into expeditions and some of them would go off into Indian country for beaver, while yet others spent their time (and risking their lives) trading with the Indians.

It was common knowledge during those early days that if whiskey peddlers and trappers were foolish enough to journey past Eagle Creek, about 25 miles downstream from Fort Benton on the Missouri, they would run the risk of meeting up with the Piegans who were camped in that part of the country. They vowed to kill any white man who dared trespass on their campgrounds.

But the money was worth the risk, and some men did, indeed, make money. However, many met with a brutal death at the hands of the Indians. As the white man showed no mercy to captured Indians, in likewise fashion neither did the Indian with the white man. This vicious cycle would continue until the end of the Nez Perce war of 1877, when peace finally was achieved. But Johnston interpreted stern warnings as an open invitation to cross Indian lands. His reputation had spread among the tribes and the Indians tended to leave him alone.

Johnston's bootleg business frequently took him across the famous "whoop-up" trail that extended north traversing the Blackfoot Indian Reservation. Johnston distributed his whiskey to "whiskey forts" with such names as Fort Spitzee, Oldham, Belly, and High Rivers, in what is now the Province of Alberta, Canada, some of which he helped construct.

Fort Benton, in north central Montana, also became headwaters for steamboat navigation. At Fort Benton, the Missouri River was shallower than at most places on the river. So the steamboats had to be constructed to accommodate the shallow waters, hence the creation of the "shallow-bottomed" steamboats.

Fort Benton was the stopping off point for people coming from St. Louis. All sorts of people clamored on board the steamships in order to reach Benton: criminals, gamblers, miners, roughnecks, ministers and prostitutes.

Most made it to Fort Benton safely, but usually only half or less actually made the return trip to St. Louis, choosing to remain in Montana Territory to look for gold, establish a business, test their gambling skills, sell their bodies, and a hundred other ways to earn a living. Some poor souls wound up dead from an Indian's bullet or well-placed arrow.

Crossing "Whoop-Up" Country

The Whoop-up country was a desolate, extremely dangerous place. Rational men avoided the area, even if they rode in large groups. But it seems that Johnston was allowed free access within its borders. An interesting story about a chance meeting between a former Army scout and Liver-Eating Johnston provides confirmation that Johnston did spend time in present day Alberta, Canada:

"While scouting through the whoop-up country (Great Falls to old Fort McLeod in British Columbia, the whoop-up country lies in northern Montana just east of Glacier Park and runs to Canada), we bumped into the old pioneer Liver-Eating Johnston, who jogged along with us for a while. He said he was just sort of 'pi-utin' around, and he certainly had room to do so, for there was not another soul in sight, and it was a notoriously bad region, where everybody got whooped up, both red men and white. One of our scouts told me that Johnston was safe anywhere, *for the Indians were superstitious about him, and kept out of range of the big telescope rifle he carried* (emphasis mine). It was also said that he really did not eat the Indian's liver, but had merely drawn it across his mouth so that the other Sioux could see and think he had eaten it after shooting an Indian and jumping over the breastworks at Fort Pease and cutting the liver. Liver-Eating Johnston hated Indians and was given the nick name, because of his threat to eat the liver of any Indian who came near his place." (90)

Such was the reputation of Liver-Eating Johnston. He was indeed a highly recognizable frontiersman, apparently having little to fear from Indians and garnering great respect from his peers.

The Lethbridge Daily Herald, May 14, 1910, a Canadian newspaper, contains an interesting article about an incident where Johnston was caught transporting whiskey to Canada. Part of the article, entitled "Standoff-Early Days of the South," is detailed below:

"Many different accounts have been given to the manner in which Standoff, near the junction of the Belly and Kootenai Rivers, on the west side of the Blood reserve, came by its name, but here is the true story. A famous character of the old days, John

Johnson, better known as "Liver-Eating" Johnson, fitted out in Montana, in company with two other men, a train of supplies, including whiskey, and started north across the South Piegan reserve in Montana to trade with the Canadian Indians. It was illegal to carry whiskey into the Piegan reserve, and a United States Marshall, getting wind of Johnson's trip, set out in pursuit with a troop of cavalry. They came up with Johnson on the reserve about 25 miles south of the international boundary and demanded his arrest. Johnson and his party promptly refused to do any such thing. They stood-off the soldiers and came on over to Belly River, and named their fort "Stand-off." (91)

Unfortunately, the article ends there. The full account of Johnston's being caught by a U.S. Marshall, as well as all of the events that occurred during this "stand off," will probably never be uncovered. But the article allows us to observe the particular, and dangerous, methods by which Johnston earned an income – legal or illegal.

The Method Used By Johnston Smuggle Whiskey

In Johnston's day, liquor was labeled "Forty-Rod." It was called forty rod because *it was the distance the drinker could run before passing out.* It was typically hauled in five-gallon kegs, astride pack mules or horses, or transported in wagons. Johnston typically transported his whiskey during the night. During the day, he hid the liquor from plain view.

How much money could be made from selling whiskey? Whiskey purchased in Montana would sell for three dollars a gallon. Peddlers like Johnston would bring the bootleg whiskey across the border in Canada and sell it for as much as *fifteen dollars* per gallon. A quart of liquor would sell for about five dollars, and a shot of whiskey, about fifty cents.

Johnston, like all other whiskey runners, traveled down a long dirt road known as "Turkey Trail." If Johnston got caught with the whiskey, it would be confiscated and he would have been fined three hundred dollars – a large amount of money in the 1870's.

Johnston Duped By Fort Benton Saloon Keepers

As was earlier mentioned, Johnston had a problem with alcohol. An interesting article has recently surfaced that describes an incident where Johnston allowed himself to be taken advantage of:

"In 1872, Fred White came to Fort Whoop Up in Canada to Fort Benton to open a saloon and dance hall. He had been engaged in the same kind of business at Whoop Up and had made money. He heard of Fort Benton as being a lively place where money was plentiful and decided to give it a trial. He made money hand over fist. Men flocked to his place and drank and danced all night and the business of the straight saloons were well shot to pieces. Charley Rowe was running a saloon at Fort Benton at the time and he and the other saloon keepers decided that something had to be done to remedy the situation and save their businesses. They put up a job on White. 'Liver Eating' Johnson was at Fort Benton at the time. He was drunk most of the time but the boys sobered him up and dressed him up to represent a prosperous trapper and hunter from the north, then took him around introduced him to White. Johnson told White that he had 4,000 buffalo robes on the way to Fort Benton and that they would be delivered to the T.C. Power & Co. store, but that of course he couldn't get his money for them until they had arrived. Other saloon keepers in the presence of White offered to let Johnson have all the money that he wanted. Rowe pulled out a roll and said: 'Here Johnson, take all you need.' 'No, don't do anything of the kind,' said White. 'Johnson, you can have

anything you want at my place, and all you want.'
White thought he had a snap in Johnson and decided to work it for all that he was worth. Then,
Rowe and others rounded up the town and arranged
for about 150 fellows to go to White's place that
night. Johnson showed up and the first thing he did
was to order the drinks for the house. Drinks were
25 cents each, and 150 of them amounted to something. Then Rowe stepped to the bar and invited
everyone in the house to drink on him. But Johnson
pushed him aside, insisting that it was his evening
and that whatever was consumed in the way of
drinks there would be on him. Whenever anyone
else tried to buy, he did the same thing. It had been
the intention of the 'jobbers' to keep it up all night
but about two in the morning two fellows got into a
fight and one of them was injured and the gathering
dispersed. It had lasted long enough, however, for
Johnson to to run up a scandalous bill. The next
morning White went to Power's store to ask about
Johnson's buffalo robes and was told that Johnson
was a drunken loafer who had no buffalo robes and
no credit at that store. White was crushed. He felt
like he didn't have a friend in the world. He began
to pack up his stuff within a week and very shortly
closed his Fort Benton place and went elsewhere.
He afterwards lived in Helena for a time." (92)

During his whiskey peddling "career," Johnston undoubtedly make quite a bit of money selling illegal liquor.
However, after perhaps three or four years of peddling,
Johnston quit the business to again pursue frontier life as a
trapper and U.S. Army scout (during the 1876-1877 Indian
Wars). The upcoming chapter discusses Johnston's participation in both pursuits.

Picture 26
"Fort Whoop-Up" whiskey fort on the Oldham River
Alberta, Canada

A
LIVER–EATING JOHNSTON
FACTOID

SPITZEE WHISKEY FORT

Liver-Eating Johnston partnered with a man named Dave Akers in order to establish the Spitzee whiskey fort in Alberta, Canada, in the early 1870's. The Blackfoot destroyed the fort soon after it was built. Johnston and Akers then went on to construct Fort Whoop-Up, which was eventually shut down by the North West Mounted Police in 1874.

8

A Country of Broken Character

The Great Indian Wars

At fifty years of age, Johnston gave up his arduous and dangerous life as a whiskey peddler. Indian activity was increasing and there were signs that the U.S. Army was about to become more aggressive in opening up the west.

Johnston Serves as Guide in 1874

Immediately after Johnston gave up whiskey peddling, he resumed performing what he knew best – trapping, hunting and serving as scout and guide for various groups. Despite the depth of his problems, Johnston was highly regarded as a man who could be relied on to take a party to the destination they requested. In particular, he probably knew the south-central/south-eastern section of Montana better than anyone did.

Interestingly, Johnston was also sometimes referred as "Jack Johnston." In 1874, Johnston and another guide, George Johnson, escorted a group interested in searching for gold into the Bighorn Mountains. In an autobiography written by long-time Johnston friend and fellow scout, Vic Smith, Smith reported that during Johnston's escorting mission to the Bighorns that Johnston's party fought off the Indians every day for nearly three months. The outfit lost only one man, while the Indians were 150 shy at the end of the game. (93)

Johnston Signs As Contract Scout With General Miles

In 1876, the year Johnston signed on to serve as scout for General Nelson A. Miles, he was already fifty-two years of age. But his chronological age shared little with the true power and fitness of his mighty frame. Even in the cross hairs of middle age, Johnston remained one of the strongest men and most prolific trappers on the western frontier.

Cast among the treachery and savagery of his Indian foe, Johnston always came out on top. Despite the often-large numbers of Indian foe who eagerly sought his prized scalp, none ever succeeded in more than sending a bullet through his thigh.

Johnston's friend, the man who was to become Coulson, Montana Territory's second deputy sheriff, was a respected frontiersman named "Muggins" Taylor. He was the man who carried the dispatch from General Terry to General Sheridan, telling of Custer's defeat. Muggins had been a scout for Terry during the battle of Little Big Horn, and was the first white man to give an account of the Custer "massacre."

Johnston did not fight at Little Big Horn. But four months later he was attached to General Nelson A. Miles, serving as a civilian scout. After Custer's defeat, the Indian bands had little time to celebrate. Hundreds of Northern Cheyenne had merged with the Sioux war chief Crazy Horse in the Powder River country in hopes of gaining another victory over the white soldiers.

The combined Indian forces battled the troopers, but this time they were soundly defeated and driven back by Colonel Wesley Merritt's 5th Cavalry at War Bonnet Creek in July of 1876. The beaten Cheyenne decided they had enough, and forged a hasty retreat to the nearby Red Cloud Agency.

During the Civil War, the highly regarded Merritt was promoted to Brigadier General due to "gallant and meritorious service" during the Brandy Station and Upperville actions of the campaign through Pennsylvania. Formerly a Captain, Merrit's promotion was very unusual. Merritt was similarly promoted to Brigadier General during the Indian Wars.

The Next Indian Confrontation

The Indian Wars' progression was next focused on a battle in September of 1876. This time it was the Civil War veteran General George Crook meeting Sioux chief American Horse and his braves at Slim Buttes. American Horse was mortally wounded during this battle, which resulted in the surrender of his men to General Crook.

Johnston Enters the Fracas

As mentioned above, John Johnston decided to contract as a scout four months after Custer was defeated at the Little Big Horn. One can only speculate what was his precise reason for scouting, but money talks. Scouting was certainly a dangerous, but well paid, profession. As a contracted scout, getting into combat was optional. Johnston was there to scout. If the Indians it took it to him, he had no choice but to fight.

Johnston was still living at the Crow Agency at Stillwater, Montana Territory, when he decided to scout again – this time for General Nelson A. Miles. As he had done for many years, Johnston would come and go from the Crow agency while scraping a living out of whatever came his way.

Miles put the word out that he wanted to be surrounded by only the best scouts. He had orders to be vigilant for Indians and to begin plans for building a cantonment to house his troopers and supplies. He wanted men who knew the country's topography and who had experience fighting Indians. So, within a short time:

"Miles gathered around him a band of old-time frontiersmen as scouts that filled the bill to a nicety. There was Liver-Eating Johnson (Jack Johnson), George Johnson, Vic Smith, Tom Cushine, Bob and Billy Jackson, Bat Shane, George Fleury, and Milan Tripp." (94)

Another incident involving Johnston also occurred during late fall/early winter of 1876-1877. Miles and his command marched up the Tongue River to the Wolf Mountains where they ran into Crazy Horse and his warriors. It was reported that:

> "a skirmish ensued and the scouts, headed by Liver-Eating Johnston, captured a buck and a squaw. Several soldiers were killed, and after the war was over the Indians admitted they had only lost one man, Big Crow, the Medicine Man." (95)

General Nelson A. Miles' command, the 5th Infantry and the 22nd Infantry, was comprised of 436 officers and men, besides five white scouts (including Yellowstone Kelly, Thomas LeForge, Liver-Eating Johnson, Robert Jackson and John Bruguier), two Crows, and one Bannock named Buffalo Horn. (96) Additional scouts were often hired by Miles on an "as needed" basis.

Miles Faces A Strong Indian Presence

General Miles was fully aware that the entire hostile force of the five Indian tribes would soon face him in battle. The Hunkpapas under Sitting Bull; the Oglallas under Crazy Horse; the Northern Cheyenne under Two Moons and the Minneconjous and Sans Arcs under their appointed leaders A strong Indian force would soon be mounting a strong attack.

Miles purposed to enter battle in the winter because he felt that the Indians would not expect white men to initiate a military campaign during the frigid winter. General Terry, Miles' superior, thought it impossible for soldiers to mount a successful fight against Indians who were thoroughly used to survival in the dead of winter.

But Miles' arguments won Terry over to his strategy, and he was given permission to begin making plans for the impending brutal winter conditions he and his men would face.

Picture 27
A Civil War Photograph of General Nelson A. Miles

Picture 28
The Superb Scout
Luther S. "Yellowstone" Kelly
This photograph explains Johnston's jealousy of Kelly

It is difficult to fathom how horrendous the weath.
in the dead of winter. Blizzards, ice storms, and fierce v
tore at the men. Add to this the roving bands of Indi
more accustomed to the rigors of winter more than Miles'
soldiers, all made the Indian Wars an extremely difficult
endeavor for both soldier and Indian.

Building the 1876 winter "Cantonment"

In order for Miles and his troopers to find some level of
comfort and protection from the horrid winter conditions,
Miles began the construction of a "fort," or cantonment, the
site of which was previously determined by one of Miles
officers. The actual location of the cantonment was at the
junction of the Tongue River and the Yellowstone. It was a
perfect location for a fort, providing quick access to the river
and serving as a jumping off point for the Indian campaign.
The men of the 5th Infantry began to cut timber and transport
logs into the selected cantonment site so that they could
build huts for both sheltering the men and storing supplies.
General Miles believed that if the Indian could survive in
"skin tents," certainly his men could survive in their wooden
huts.

Miles' Campaign Begins

Miles was in pursuit of hostile Sioux who had escaped
north. He was at a considerable advantage because he knew
that a tough winter fight would either force the Sioux to
reconcile with the Army or force them far north in Canada.
In his autobiography, Yellowstone Kelly stated how difficult
it would be for the Sioux to maintain strength in the face of
rigorous winter pursuit by well-fed, well-armed U.S. Army
troops:

> "Your wild Indian in order to live comfortably must
> camp where there is game and (food) for his pony
> herds and where the women can dress hides to bar-

ter for flour, cloth, powder and shell ammunition, salt, and sugar." (97)

Miles knew that the "hostiles" would be kept considerably off-balance by his pursuit and that, in order to survive, must head toward established hunting grounds where they could replenish supplies and gain much needed rest. These hunting grounds were generally in the area where Johnston maintained his wood yard - certainly familiar territory to the crafty Liver-Eater.

Dealing with the Torturous Montana Winters

Johnston and the men of the 5th had to endure the frightful Montana winters. Many men felt that alcohol would help ward off the gloomy effects of Arctic-like conditions and temper the anxiety each man faced in anticipation of meeting the hostile Indians.

When the cantonment was finally completed, a problem arose with the sale of rum and other alcohol. Three different traders, with businesses at the cantonment, sold alcohol to Miles' men. Miles had permitted the consumption of malted liquors, beer and wine (limited to only a few drinks a day), hoping somehow to moderate the amount of alcohol consumed by each man.

One trader made his own gin in his cellar, which tragically poisoned some of Miles' command. It got so bad that the guardhouse was continually packed with drunken soldiers.

Miles finally removed the liquor traders, but it did little good. The soldiers simply took their trade to where the traders had set up their new businesses outside of the fort's confines.

But the most difficult reality with which Johnston and the others had to confront was the bitter cold. Proper winter clothing was scarce, so the men had to devise their own protective clothing to keep warm. Jerome Greene, in his fine book "Yellowstone Command," states that: "Some soldiers fashioned blanket suits that proved comfortable, while most protected their heads from the icy blasts with caps with earflaps. Some soldiers fabricated protection for their face by creating facemasks with openings for eyes and mouth. Many wore canvas leggings, often blanket lined, made from shelter items. Blankets were cut into assorted garb, including underclothing and trousers, while duck overalls safeguarded many soldiers from the cold." (98)

The conditions were so extreme that during the winter campaign of 1876 and 1877, Miles' mercury thermometers had frozen solid. A spirit thermometer recorded temperatures between 55 and 60 degrees below zero. It was so cold that the air was filled with tiny shining crystals.

Johnston Meets the Enemy

One of Johnston's first fights was with the combined force of Sioux and Cheyenne in December of 1876. Chief of Scouts Kelly ordered Johnston and four other scouts, as well as several Indian scouts, to investigate a report of a massing of hostiles up the northern side of the Tongue River near their camp.

The scouts raced to where the enemy was located, observing several warriors on a ridge. As the scouts moved toward the small party of Sioux, they quickly noticed that there were actually fifteen Indians hiding further down the slope of the ridge.

Kelly decided to charge the group. To his surprise, he was met with nearly fifty of the enemy who had cleverly concealed themselves and began firing at the scouts. Kelly and his men returned fire; at the same time turning their horses around to head toward the timber line a short distance behind them.

In order to reach a secure defensive position, the scouts had to coerce their horses to jump down a six-foot depression with hopes of landing on solid ground upon which the men could establish a defensive position. Riding on a bit more, the men finally stopped their horses and took a stand.

The Sioux and Cheyenne respected the marksmanship of the scouts and never exposed themselves openly to gunfire. They fired randomly, taking no effort to aim at a target. Up to one hundred Indians now gathered in their attack against the small band of scouts.

Word got back to General Miles that his scouts were pinned down by Indian gunfire. He decided to send out a detachment of soldiers up the valley to aid the scouts. In addition, Miles had his artillery fire a shot at some Indians who were standing on a rise near Kelly's position.

This seemed to do the trick. Another artillery shell was fired over the scouts' head, splitting up the Indians and spreading them out. Finally, the infantry was seen making fast headway to the battle scene, and the scouts moved quickly to safety.

With the scouts and infantry back at camp, evening drew. There was some occasional gunfire exchanged, but the Sioux and Cheyenne moved their force back to re-group in anticipation of an early morning attack.

Early morning brought a swift fight. Furious fighting began immediately. Miles' soldiers poured lead into the Indian attack, while Kelly and his scouts "took a break" from the action and observed the attack, leaving the fighting to Miles and his men. Scouts Kelly and Johnston were hired to serve as guides, not to necessarily "enter the fray."

The General ordered for the artillery piece, a three-inch howitzer, to be used to disrupt the enemy position. The howitzer quickly became a target for Indian marksmen.

Miles then sent two companies of men toward the enemy, driving them back down the ridge from whence they came. The Sioux and Cheyenne made haste to retreat up the Tongue River, with their goal of reaching the protection of Wolf Mountain.

Johnston Nearly Killed

In the midst of the furious action, Johnston came near to being killed. According to Jerome Greene, Johnston was with Captain Casey, who took some men and a field gun across a frozen stream to charge the Indians. The fighting extended into the evening, but no Indians were killed.

One unofficial report extracted by Greene from the diary of a trooper named Brown, reported that "... Liver-Eating Johnson had had a furrow cut through his long hair: he said it was close." (99)

Johnston was involved in many campaigns with the Indians. He participated in the battles of Muddy Creek, Bark Creek, Cedar Creek, Ash Creek and Spring Creek.

Picture 29
A Cheyenne Scalping

The Nez Perce War of 1877

As the Sioux and Cheyenne Wars were coming to an end, conflicts with the Nez Perce were just beginning. Liver-Eating Johnston played a role in the conflict.

Johnston was one of several scouts hired during the summer of 1877 to guide Army troops through the wilderness. With Miles, Howard and Sturgis in the field, all trying to capture Chief Joseph, good scouts were in demand.

For every small squad detached from the three columns operating against the Indians, a guide was mandated. With Yellowstone Kelly getting the brunt of the recognition as the "best" scout, it was known that Johnston was at times jealous of Kelly's favor with General Miles. Perhaps it was the fact that Kelly was articulate, educated, clean and sociable - the antithesis of Johnston. Nevertheless, Johnston remained a fine and loyal scout - equal to Kelly in skill and cunning.

The Nez Perce was the tribe who extended gracious hospitality to Lewis and Clark during their expedition. They prided themselves on never having killed a white man. They were even tolerant of the white settlers, who, during the 1850's, pushed them from their sacred homelands.

Several stories provide a suggestion of how the Nez Perce war began. One story states that the Nez Perce war began when a drunken warrior named Shore Crossing, still angry at the whites for killing his father several years earlier, decided to seek vengeance. Taking along another Nez Perce brave with the idea of shedding blood, Shore Crossing left his camp seeking whites to murder. He found a small party of men, killing two and wounding one.

Not satisfied with just two killings, sixteen other Nez Perce later joined Shore Crossing and murdered other innocent people. Chief Joseph knew it was inevitable that war would soon come to the Nez Perce.

The killing of innocent whites brought Chief Joseph to the realization that there was now no turning back. Joseph uprooted his people and moved to White Bird Canyon, where he sought concealment from the Army.

Another story suggested that a young warrior, whose brother had been killed by a white man, exacted revenge on the man who had killed his sibling. The warrior murdered the white man and stole his horse.

Regardless of how the Nez Perce War began, there was no turning back for Chief Joseph and his people. Joseph was determined to escape and take his people to safety. But the Army quickly discovered them.

The Nez Perce leader, Chief Joseph, and his small band of warriors, soundly defeated the soldiers as they tried to uproot the tenacious Indians. Realizing that the soldiers would soon be upon them again in full force, they moved their entire village into, and across, the Bitterroot Mountains and headed toward Canada, and then hopefully to safety.

General Oliver O. Howard resolutely chased Chief Joseph and his now diminished band of warriors, women and children, as they raced for the Canadian border. The historic pursuit of Joseph took the soldiers on a 1,700-mile chase, finally stopping the Nez Perce only 40 miles from Canada.

It was finally Colonel Nelson A. Miles who trapped Joseph. Liver-Eating Johnston and the rest of Miles' scouts are recorded by historians as being key to the final capture of the Nez Perce band. Johnston also scouted for General Samuel Sturgis, who had lost a son (Lt. James Sturgis), at the Little Big Horn battle.

Sturgis led his command across Rocky Creek in order to go to Miles' relief fearing that Sitting Bull might come to the rescue of some Sioux Indians whom Miles had captured. It was thought that Miles had intercepted the Nez Perce, so Sturgis made his way with his entire command to find Miles to determine if indeed there had been a fight.

Sturgis chose Johnston as guide and everything depended upon him, for no one else in the command knew anything about the country that the command had to traverse. With little haste, Johnston began to lead the command to its destination, intuitively determining where Miles' command was located.

Picture 30
General Oliver O. Howard

Johnston served as scout for Howard. Two gunshot wounds
caused Howard's right arm to be amputated during the
Civil War.

Picture 31
General Samuel Sturgis

Liver-Eating Johnston Served As One of His Scouts
During the Nez Perce War Campaign. Sturgis Praised
Johnston's Scouting Abilities.

Johnston's scouting was based upon his knowledge of the country and patterns of terrain that Johnston believed Miles would use for either an offensive or defensive stand.

Another Unusual Name for Johnston

Charles Wood, an officer, recorded an interesting incident involving Johnston. As an aide-de-camp with the 5th Infantry, serving with General Miles during the Nez Perce war, Wood had an opportunity to meet Johnston on October 4, 1877. It appeared that many people were impressed enough with Johnston that they felt the necessity to record meetings they had with him. The following is a good example:

> "At earliest daylight of the 4th of October we resumed our quest of Miles, still following the Indian trail. In the afternoon we saw a man at a distance across the prairie, evidently puzzled by our appearance. General Howard sent a couple of our scouts to bring him in. He turned out to be a bearer of mail and dispatches from Miles' post at Fort Keogh, and he was trying to find him. He was a frontiersman called *Slippery Dick* or 'Liver-Eating Johnson' because, by his own story and popular report, he was supposed to have eaten a piece of the liver of an Indian whom had killed and scalped..." (100)

The End of the Great Indian Wars

Two major events effectively ended the Indian Wars - the surrender of the Nez Perce leader, Chief Joseph, on October 5, 1877, at Bear Paw Mountains; and General Terry's efforts at bringing peace with Sitting Bull, who was still a refugee living in Canada for nearly a year. There would be no major outbreaks from Sitting Bull while he was living in Canada. But there would be legitimate scares when, for example, some

Sioux crossed the border to hunt on Assiniboin land. Colonel Miles was forced to escort them back to Canada.

Also, some bands of Sioux were raiding civilian targets near Bismark and Fort Keogh, stealing horses and cattle. However, on July 19, 1881, a starving Sitting Bull rode into Fort Buford with a small band of Hunkpapa Sioux, and surrendered. As Jerome Greene stated, "...the surrender of Sitting Bull symbolized the conclusion of three decades of confrontation between the government and the Sioux." (101)

Liver-Eating Took Breaks From Scouting

Because Johnston was an "independent contractor," he could come and go as he pleased, dress as he pleased, and work when he pleased. When not scouting, Johnston typically did what he loved best – hunting and trapping. For example, in the autobiography written by fellow scout and Johnston friend Vic Smith, mention was made about one of many occasions when he Johnston went hunting:

> "(Vic) left the Crow mission the last of January 1877 and returned to Fort Keogh. He quit scouting for a while and went wolfing with Jack (Liver-Eating) and George Johnson about twenty-five miles from the fort in February and March. Tom Keefe went along, and in six weeks they had more than six hundred wolves. Ninety-four were killed in one night at the carcass of one buffalo (poisoned with strychnine)."(102)

Johnston Becomes a Yellowstone Scout

There were other incidents that involved Johnston as a scout with the U.S. Army. In one of these incidents, the Nez Perce began to retreat down the Clark Fork to the Yellowstone River Valley in early September of 1877. The Nez Perce had killed several miners along Clarks Fork, stealing their horses. The Nez Perce then raided the house of J.M.V.

Cochran, where two trappers, guests of Cochran's, were killed.

Joseph MV Cochran c1916

Picture 32
"Yellowstone Scout" JMV Cochran

In addition, some warriors rode into the town of Coulson and burned the saloon. Because of these acts, Cochran and Liver-Eating Johnston became members of Lt. George Houston's *Yellowstone Scouts.* (103)

Johnston was fifty-three years of age during this event - still highly capable of vigorous physical activity. Serving as scout at his age took an outstanding amount of both mental and physical strength. Being in the saddle, being exposed to the elements, sleeping out in the cold, the fear of Indian attacks, all combined to make Johnston a highly unusual "senior citizen."

Author Mark H. Brown describes another account of Johnston joining the Yellowstone Scouts:

"Howard (General) engaged a prospector named George Houston for a guide, and enlisted about twenty others as scouts in a body called the 'Yellowstone Scouts...'" (104)

Finally, there is one more account relating to Johnston's participation as scout: "...after the attack (by the Nez Perce), Joseph Cochran left the area with Liver Eating Johnson to join with General O.O. Howard's command near Pompey's Pillar. He became one of the Yellowstone Scouts." (105)

Johnston Scouts Against the Cheyenne – May 1877

When Johnston decided to scout again, he contracted with his old employer, Colonel Nelson A. Miles. It was late spring and Miles detected a band of about fifty Sioux and Cheyenne warriors on the Rosebud River. The duty was given to Jack (Liver-Eating) Johnston, George Johnson, Vic Smith and Bob Jackson, to scout ahead. Future sheriff, and Johnston employer, Tom Irvine, was also a scout during this Rosebud campaign.

Liver-Eating Johnston and the scouts decided to ride into the middle of the Indian camp, guiding their horses between the teepees and the large herd of grazing horses.

The scouts managed to steal the herd and rush them away down the valley. The warriors were cut off from their horses and ran to the nearby hills.

It was obvious that the fight was already taken out of some of the Indians. Even their two chiefs, Lame Deer and Iron Star, didn't run, preferring to wait on Miles' entry into the camp.

In a murderous rage, Lame Deer and Iron Star were shot and killed by the scout Bob Jackson, and then scalped in view of Miles, who is reported to have turned away in disgust. All told, the battle took the lives of fourteen Indians and four of Miles' men. The final count for horses recovered by Miles' men was near one thousand, which reportedly the Sioux stole back a short time later.

Newspaper Accounts of Liver-Eating Johnston's Participation in the Indian Wars

Several accounts exist of Johnston's activities during the 1876-1877 Indian Wars. Former officers under whom Johnston had served wrote the contents of the accounts, for the most part. It is a tribute to the skills of Johnston that his commanders took time to comment upon his contributions as scout during the Indian Wars.

The following reference about Johnston is written word for word as they appeared in either period newspapers or in other references containing military memoirs of former Johnston commanders.

Major General Hugh Scott's Account

"We were camped on a silted-up channel of the Missouri, which made a beautiful sward, without brush or rose-bushes, the edges dotted here and there with giant cottonwood, five or six feet in diameter, reminding one of an English park. The weather was quite cold, and at night we would all gather around a huge fire to listen to stories from the scouts, mainly from Liver-Eating Johnson, who was said to have eaten a piece of an Indian's liver in a fit of bravado. His language was very quaint, and we would often listen to him until one o'clock in the morning. He was a tall, powerful man with a hairy torso like that of a bull. He carried a sixteen-pound buffalo Sharp's rifle, which, with its belt of ammunition was a load for any ordinary man. He would leave camp on foot and soon kill and dress an antelope, cutting off its head and tying all four feet together. This he would swing over his shoulder like a sack, the body under his left arm, and go on and kill another, to be swung under the right arm. Billy Jackson was a Blackfoot, who had been a scout for the Seventh Cavalry the year before, and had been cut off in the timber with De Rudio, Gerard, and Sgt. O'Neill, and left behind by Reno during the battle at the Little Big Horn. Jackson had wintered in Lincoln, Rice, and Standing Rock, and I had thought in those days that he was a Sioux halfbreed. He had come up the Missouri with us as far as Fort Keogh, where I had missed him until meeting him here. His brother, Bob Jackson was with him, but not nearly so good a man. When Bob Jackson and Liver-Eating Johnston left our camp, it may have been a mere coincidence that a bunch of our horses left the same night." (106)

So...Johnston was suspected of stealing horses from General Scott's command. His actions speak volumes.

A
LIVER-EATING JOHNSTON
FACTOID

LUTHER S. "YELLOWSTONE" KELLY

Yellowstone Kelly served as chief-of-scouts for General Nelson A. Miles during the Indian Wars of 1876-1877. From time to time, Johnston was under Kelly's command. Kelly wanted to meet General Miles, so, instead of a calling card, Kelly sent Miles a severed bear's paw. Miles was impressed by Yellowstone Kelly's "creativity."

9

The Montana Lawman

In July of 1879, the summer after Johnston's exploits at the Hoskin & McGirl trading post, the Liver-Eater had reached his fifty-fifth birthday. Although still massive and in excellent physical condition, he nevertheless suffered from the trapper's malady- rheumatism.

Concurrently, and unbeknownst to Johnston, he was also developing heart disease, i.e., arteriosclerosis, which would eventually contribute to his death in January of 1900, although his death certificate stated that he died of peritonitis.

Johnston Pursues Scouting, Trapping and Hunting

Authoritative speculation has Johnston continuing what he knew best – seeking animal hides and guiding individuals and groups to their contracted destinations.

As can be expected, there is a general absence of biographical material for Johnston from 1880 to 1882 to verify this postulate, but it is with certainty that Liver-Eating Johnston continued to make ends meet by pursuing what he'd followed all his life – hunting and trapping.

Johnston Runs a Stage Coach Line

One reference exists which reported that Johnston was involved in a local stagecoach business. During the years 1877- 1881, Johnston "maintained a stage coach station in the Pease Bottom country and later at a place near Billings. Pease was a trading and trapping station." (107) Johnston was still involved in the Nez Perce war until October of 1877 when Chief Joseph surrendered. It is, however, possible that Johnston began working with the stagecoach station after his scouting duties had expired. Since there is only scant mention of Johnston's activities during the time period 1877 – 1881, Johnston could have involved himself with this line of work.

Picture 33
John Liver-Eating Johnston at age 58 (1882).
His powerful frame is evident in this photograph.

The Emergence of Coulson, Montana Territory

The laying of tracks in Montana for the Northern Pacific Rail Road (NPRR) began in October of 1881 when the construction crews entered Montana. During the month of July, on the 22nd, it was reported that the NPRR was only twenty-three miles from Billings. Finally, on August 22nd, 1882, the NPRR track-laying crew reached the area of Billings, and was greeted with an enthusiastic reception from its townspeople. (108)

The area that we now know as Billings, Montana, was well known by Johnston. It sat upon the traditional land of the Mountain Crow Indians. It was also the spot near where, in 1877, an enterprising businessman named P.W. McAdow established a trading post and stage station. (109)

However, before the tent town of Billings existed, the town of Coulson sprung to life in 1877. It was located on the north bank of the Yellowstone River, and called "Coulson" by McAdow in honor of S.B. Coulson. S.B. Coulson was the general manager of the Coulson Steamboat Company, which owned the Josephine, (piloted by Johnston's old friend Grant Marsh) and several other boats.

By naming the town Coulson, McAdow hoped that he could butter-up Mr. Coulson in order to entice him to have his steamboats make stops in the new town named after him. The fledgling town boasted a post office, a brewery, several general stores, a telegraph office, a dance hall, other businesses and several saloons. The town's founder, McAdow, had good expectations for Coulson. (110)

Coulson's location was well thought out. It sat on the Yellowstone River, which permitted steamboats and other vessels to supply the town and outlying areas with the goods and products citizens required. The town was wide open, and began to attract people less inclined to settle down into a life of civility and purpose.

Picture 34
Coulson, Montana Territory, 1882
Liver-Eating Johnston Walked These Streets and
Busted Heads as Sheriff

"Jack" Johnston – Justice of the Peace

Liver-Eating Johnston's first foray as an officer of the law began in late 1881. According to Dr. Lorman L. Hoopes' book, "This Last West," the Custer County Board of Commissioners appointed Johnston justice of the peace for Custer County on December 24, 1881. He undoubtedly was "stationed" in Miles City with his old friend and fellow army scout, Sheriff (and Assessor) of Custer County, Montana Territory, Tom Irvine.

Tom Irvine, like Johnston, was an independent scout for General Miles in October of 1876, serving at the Rosebud in

1877. After the Indian Wars ended, Irvine was appointed Constable of Miles Township, Montana, on January 7, 1878.

Irvine was also a friend of "X". Beidler, who himself lived in Miles Township for a short while. In September of 1881, Tom Irvine begins his new duties as Sheriff and Assessor of Custer County.

There is no date as to when Johnston first arrived in Coulson prior to his being hired as County Deputy in November 1882. However, it was recorded that after the murder of Muggins Taylor (October 1882), Johnston became one of the new county deputies. (111)

There appears to be some confusion among writers and historians about the length of time Johnston spent as a lawman in the towns of Coulson/Billings. Let it be known, that Johnston remained as a lawman until he joined the Hardwick Wild West Show in 1884.

The Northern Pacific Railroad had reached Billings on August 22nd, 1882. Irvine needed a strong hand at Coulson and Billings to handle the railroad crews. Johnston was encouraged to leave his position as justice of the peace and run for deputy sheriff.

By the time Johnston took the reins of justice, there had already been about 25 deaths by gunshot in the town of Coulson alone since the town's beginnings in 1877. It was said of Johnston that he didn't need any weapons to keep the peace. It had further been reported that he either kicked troublemakers in their rump or simply knocked them out with a punch.

Johnston's ability to maintain peace resided in his established reputation as an Indian fighter, his fearlessness and his prodigious strength. His friend, Ben Greenough, wrote that people believed Johnston was "the strongest man in Montana Territory."(112)

Picture 35
A Confident Liver-Eating Johnston.

<u>Riding the Rails - 1882</u>

The following story helps to further construct a chronology of Johnston's activities during the early 1880's. Below is described an incident involving a young man's confrontation with Johnston aboard an Oregon Short Line train. The incident was recorded in a book written in 1905 featuring a young man named Charles Pickway, who encountered Liver-Eating Johnston and his "gang," as both parties rode a train heading for Idaho. The intriguing, full story is included below:

"...after fording mountain streams and crossing rugged divides, Mr. Pickway arrived at Leadville (Colorado) with only a few dollars left. He at once was taken sick with mountain fever and lay for one week hovering between life and death at the County hospital. When he recovered he returned to Denver. He secured work on the Oregon Short Line, which was then under construction, and which furnished transportation to Pocatello, Idaho. As the train was passing through Wyoming, a gang of desperados and cowboys got on at Bitter Creek bound for the Wood River country in Idaho. At Ogden all had to change cars and get into box cars. Pickway was put in a box car with those desperados, and as soon as the train started they commenced to drink, curse and shoot. Pickway was scared almost to death. The leader of the gang, called Liver-Eating Johnson (because it was said he had killed an Indian and eaten his liver), was the toughest looking character Pickway had ever seen. Johnson said some one had stolen one of his shirts, and he commenced to swear and shoot. He said if he could find out who took his shirt he would make a sieve out of him. Johnson and his gang (began) to search the car. Pickway knew he had not taken Johnson's shirt. He commenced to hop and yell for blood. He cocked both his revolvers and wanted to know who owned those blankets. Pickway saw the only hope for him to escape without being killed was to get out the end door as soon as possible, but as soon as he started to they all shouted 'there goes the thief!' Johnson (began) to shoot as Pickway was going between the cars. Two of the men grabbed him and pulled him back, and Johnston said to him 'I will give you three minutes to pray before I kill you.' Pickway got down on his knees at once and commenced to pray and asked God to help him. He said that he had not stolen the shirt. He asked God to help his poor mother, for 'he was going to be killed.' The gang of desperados went on to Black Foot, Idaho, and crossed the Idaho desert into the Wood River Country. Pickway went on to the American Falls on the Snake River, which was the end of the track of the Oregon Short Line at that time. He only worked about ten days unloading ties and went to Montana, where the Northern Pacific was then building. He went to work in a tie-camp at fifty dollars per month and board." (113)

The Oregon Short Line (OSL) was tied in with the Union Pacific Rail Road. Construction on the OSL began in July of 1881, starting with a ceremony at Granger, Wyoming

Construction crews slowly moved westward, sticking with the path of the Oregon Trail. On August 2, 1882, the OSL was incorporated in the territories of Utah, Idaho, and Oregon. No specific date was attached to this Pickway incident, but a good guess would be in *late fall of 1882*. Construction crews for the Northern Pacific had already entered Montana in December 1881, about the same time Johnston was hired as justice of the peace for Custer County.

The year of 1882 would have found Liver-Eating Johnston to be about fifty-eight years of age (he was born in 1824). The Indian Wars had essentially concluded in 1877 with the surrender of Chief Joseph and the Nez Perce (a relatively inactive Sitting Bull would surrender in 1881). It certainly seems apparent that Johnston was unsettled even during his late fifties. However, his wanderlust would soon end in a most surprising way shortly after his train-riding days were concluded.

Johnston Settles Down

As far as can be ascertained, Johnston did not move near a so-called "city" until he became county deputy in Coulson, Montana, in or about 1882. Even as a lawman, Johnston fervently clung to his old ways. An article written in 1889 described Johnston's preference for wearing his traditional mountain man clothing while walking the streets of the towns for who he served as justice of the peace, county deputy sheriff, or constable:

> "...in dress, looks, and general outline, he (Johnston) is the typical character of the early hunter and trapper, and glories in the fact that the onward march of civilization has failed to make any impression on his frontier modes and habits of life. His hair and beard are still long and shaggy, and for wearing apparel he still clings with the greatest tenacity to the skins of wild beasts, like the untutored savage." (114)

Johnston Eats Thirteen Buffalo – All By Himself

Johnston was known to possess an enormous appetite. It was reported that his craving for meat was phenomenal. The following stories about Liver-Eating's incredible ability to eat massive amounts of food (which ultimately led to heart disease) were related by the late Harry Owens, of Red Lodge, Montana:

> "During one particular winter, while wolfing on Marias River, northwest of present Great Falls,

Montana he (Johnston) killed and ate thirteen buffalo. He shot them and hung them up near his cabin at the beginning of the season. When spring came, there was very little left." (115)

Rather than debate the incredible contents of this story, the information presented is most certainly a testament to a man possessing a tremendous appetite. If Owens' description is tongue in cheek, it nevertheless is entertaining.

Another interesting story related by Owens concerning Johnston's appetite occurred at the ranch of Johnston friend, John Henry:

"One day when Fred Longmore (Owens' uncle) and his cousin Charlie Thiel, were out a John Henry's ranch, John Johnson was there too. Mrs. Henry told the boys that if they would be quiet, they could watch Johnson eat beef. A steer had been killed the day before. They weighed out a chunk of about six pounds and Mrs. Henry started to cook it in a big, black kettle. When it got hot, Johnson took a big knife and fork and a salt shaker and started to eat. By the time the kettle got a full boil, Johnson had eaten the whole chunk of meat." (116)

No Arrests by Deputy Sheriff Johnston at Coulson/Billings

If there is one story that is widely-written about and acknowledged for its uniqueness it is the fact that Liver-Eating Johnston did not carry out his law enforcement duties according to the standard police procedure of his day (what little there was of it). Johnston's own particular style of keeping the peace was "typically Johnston."

On one particular day, Sheriff Tom Irvine decided to come to Coulson by stagecoach because he had heard there was trouble in the neighborhood of "camp" Coulson. Irvine began to wonder why his deputy never reported any arrests.

Johnston was supposed to have sent prisoners to Miles City where prisoners would be placed in a cell.

Upon reaching town, Irvine met with Johnston and inquired as to the reason Johnston had sent no prisoners to Miles City. The following conversation is reportedly what occurred between the two lawmen after Irvine questioned Johnston:

> "Well you see Tom, the boys get into a scrap once in a while, but I just take two of them and bump their heads together, and that settles it. There ain't no use arrestin' 'em. I guess I can keep peace among these pilgrims." (117)

Johnston Transports Six Prisoners By Himself in 1882

An article in the Coulson-Billings Post (June 16, 1882), tells of a typical day in Johnston's life as a lawman:

> "Deputy Sheriff Johnson passed through on the stage en route to Deer Lodge with six sentenced prisoners in charge, one of whom has engaged board and room for 30 years, his crime being murder in the second degree. This trip of one deputy with six prisoners from Miles City to Deer Lodge sounded like quite a feat, until it dawned upon the compiler, that the super-officer was none but the redoubtable 'Liver Eating' Johnson..." (118)

The Murder of Johnston Long-Time Friend – H.M. "Muggins" Taylor

"Muggins" Taylor received his nickname because of his favorite card game–Muggins. Taylor was Coulson's second peace officer; Johnston, its third. Joyce M. Jensen provides an excellent short biography about Taylor:

"He (Taylor) is known because he has claim to a 'piece of the Custer legend.' He was a scout with the Montana Column commanded by General John Gibbon. On June 27, 1876, he was with Gibbon's Seventh Infantry which discovered the remains of General George Custer and his men after the battle of the Little Bighorn. Taylor started to carry the news of Custer's defeat through the territory that somewhere definitely held the winners of that battle. He reached Horace Countryman's ranch (near present-day Columbus). The next day he and friend Countryman continued the ride to the closest telegraph at Fort Ellis near Bozeman, only to learn that the telegraph was unavailable. Countryman arrived in Helena in early July with the shocking news. Custer had fought on June 25, 1876. By the time the word reached the east, it was that great day of celebration, July 4, 1876- the 100th birthday, the Centennial of the United States. Who was H.M. Muggins" Taylor? He was a tailor and was frequently called upon to fashion fur coats and buckskin suits. He was a scout for the Army... He was a hunter and trapper who furnished meat to some of the early settlements in... part of the Yellowstone (region). He was a kindly, gentle man, well liked and respected. In 1882, "Muggins" Taylor was a Custer County deputy sheriff in Coulson...He went to arrest the laundress' drunken husband, Hank Lumpp (spelling of his name varies), who beat her, shot up saloons and generally caused trouble. After threatening the saloonkeeper, the drunken husband shot Taylor. Taylor was carried to Billings and...but he died of his wounds." (119)

Taylor was shot on September 28, 1882 and died on October 1, 1882. Johnston was elected deputy sheriff six weeks later on November 11, 1882. Johnston apparently served about one year and one half as deputy sheriff of Coulson and

Billings before joining Hardwick's Wild West Show where he was billed as "The Avenging Fury of the Plains" in the spring and summer of 1884.

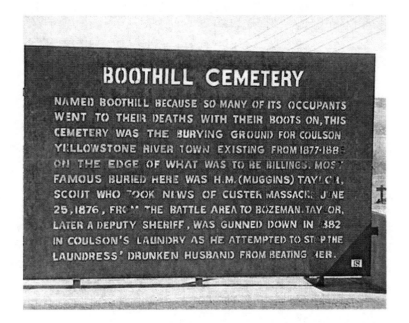

Picture 36
Muggins Taylor Grave Site
Boot Hill Memorial Cemetery

Picture 37
Indian Fighter and Johnston Friend
W.H. "Muggins" Taylor

Muggins Taylor - the Marksman

Liver-Eating Johnston's' predecessor, Muggins Taylor, had earlier won a reputation as a crack shot during battles with the Sioux at Fort Pease. Fort Pease was a trading and trapping station, located on the Yellowstone River near where the Big Horn River empties into the Yellowstone.

Thirty hunters, trappers and wolfers occupied the fort, including Taylor, X. Beidler, the McCormack brothers and Liver-Eating Johnston. It was now the winter of 1875 and the Sioux were angry partly because wolfers were using strychnine to kill wolves, and, without intent, the pet dogs of the Sioux.

There were thirty men at Fort Pease and only fourteen rifles. After a boating mishap on the Yellowstone, sixteen rifles were lost due to a capsized boat. More men than rifles spelled trouble.

While waiting for reinforcements from a town located near present day Billings, "Muggins" Taylor became a frontier legend with one shot. The story has Taylor peering out on a rise above the fort, observing the animated antics of a Sioux warrior.

"Muggins" Taylor made a long distance shot at an Indian which was little short of miraculous, and while he always modestly claimed that "it was jest [sic] a fluke shot," and that "it couldn't be done agin'[sic] on a thousand trials," the others argued that his marksmanship had more to do with it than anything else:

"Muggins was armed with a Colt repeating rifle, which had been given to him by a wealthy Eastern sportsmen who he had guided through Yellowstone Park on a hunting trip... For several successive days an Indian had appeared on an eminence at a considerable distance from the stockade, where he had gone through mocking antics and derisive gestures... Rushing to one of the portholes, where he could get a careful rest, Taylor 'drew down' on the

161

defiant figure. 'Crr-rack! W-h-a-m!' and as a cloud of smoke breezed away from the muzzle of his rifle, the interested watchers saw the Indian reel unsteadily and dizzily. Several within the stockade had field glasses trained on the distant redskin, and noted that he sank to the ground." (120)

Johnston vs. Professional Boxer

Undoubtedly Johnston was very good with his fists. A fine example of this prowess is demonstrated during the times he beat up troublemakers rather than threatening them with a gun. There is a remarkable incident recorded by the late Red Lodge resident, Harry Owens, which occurred while Johnston was a lawman in Billings.

The new town of Billings was occasionally frequented by professional boxers from the east who put on exhibitions and offered invitations to any man willing to face them in the boxing ring. Typically, challengers would be rewarded with the prize of a few dollars if they could last more than three rounds with the professional.

The townspeople of Billings knew that Johnston was quite strong and powerful. They knew that he still possessed quick reflexes, even at his age.

Owens stated that saloon owners Ryan and Flannagan relished the idea of professional boxers challenging ordinary citizens. It would be great for business, they thought. Someone recommended that the visiting boxer face Liver-Eating Johnston.

After Johnston was asked if he wanted to fight the touring boxer, Johnston agreed. After all, the Liver-Eater had honed his survival skills for nearly forty years. He was enormously confident in his abilities to handle any physical challenge.

The young professional knew nothing about Johnston. All he saw before him was a large, gray-haired man with a wildly unkempt graying beard who appeared to be about sixty years old. The pugilist must have wondered why he was fighting this old relic.

Johnston agreed to fight the boxer, but on his own terms. He wanted the fight to take place in private, not wanting it to be a public spectacle. He also wanted to fight bare-knuckled, not using the awkward boxing gloves that the professional used.

The professional agreed to fight in private. So, the fighters slowly walked to the rear of Ryan and Flanagan's' saloon. Johnston had won one concession, but so did his opponent. The Liver-Eater was forced to wear boxing gloves after all because the professional did not want to risk unnecessary injury. So, reluctantly, Johnston placed the strange, bulky equipment on his huge hands.

As the men faced each other, the professional must have thought that Johnston was an easy mark; that this bout was somehow just a novelty "set up" by the saloon owners for publicity. But he was soon to learn the fury and power of Liver-Eating Johnston. Each fighter squared off, each displaying his own unique boxing stance.

But before the professional knew what had happened, Johnston threw a lightening fast right hand that sliced through the pro's defense and knocked him through a wooden fence. Shocked and embarrassed, Johnston's opponent quickly stood up, thinking that Johnston's punch must have been a fluke.

The men squared off again, with the result being that Johnston again threw a powerful right hand, rendering the boxer unconscious before he hit the ground. After regaining consciousness, the boxer admitted that he and Johnston were clearly "not in the same league." (121)

A Summary of the Bogus Hunter's Hot Springs Photo

A picture has been bouncing around the internet for years that purportedly includes several famous old west characters. The picture includes a likeness of Liver-Eating Johnston. Turn to page 165 and look at the photograph. It

163

certainly looks legitimate, but it is, alas, an incredible "snow-job." Check out the figure standing behind "Johnston." Morgan Earp? It has to be a ghost because Morgan was murdered in Tombstone in 1882. And consider "Ben Greenough," (last man on the right, seated). He was a good friend of Johnston, but he did not arrive in Billings until 1886! The other "frontiersmen" in the photo are similarly "bogus."

Johnston's Reputation Grows

The Billings Gazette recorded other accounts about the reputation enjoyed by Johnston in the shantytown of Coulson:

> "When the stalwart form of the old pioneer loomed coming up and down the main street of Coulson, jamborees were suddenly suspended and a Connecticut Sabbath prevailed." (122)

Johnston 's Tenure Ends As Coulson's/Billing's Deputy Sheriff.

When Johnston was not re-elected as deputy sheriff in the spring of 1884, he decided to participate in a Wild West show, which unfortunately went "bust" in August of 1884. The show went bankrupt, either in Chicago, St. Paul, or a small town in Wisconsin. Out of work again, Johnston began his long trek back home to Montana. He stopped off in Minneapolis, Minnesota, to apply for an increase in his military pension for wounds suffered during the Civil War battle at Westport, Missouri.

Picture 38
Bogus Picture of Old West Personalities.
This notorious 1883 Photo *is a fake*.

Enlarged Photo
From Hunter's Hot Springs

The Real Johnston
in 1882-1883

A Clever Illusion...

Timeline – 1884

Mentioned earlier was the fact that Johnston was involved with a Wild West show. While the star of the show was the famous Custer Crow scout, Curly, Johnston also was considered as a major attraction. While conducting research for *The Avenging Fury of the Plains,* this author became friends with the late Harry Owens. Owens was a Johnston historian and was probably the first to state that Johnston was billed as "The Avenging Fury of the Plains" in a then unknown Wild West Show.

Author Joyce Jensen stated that the *Great Rocky Mountain Show* met its end in late 1884. This helps to further pin down Johnston's activities during the mid 1880's. (123)

Based upon Jensen's account, it is safe to state that Johnston left his position as deputy sheriff in the spring of 1884 to join the show.

Johnston and the Piegan Indian Raids of 1885

During the fall of 1885, small parties of the Piegan Indian nation began to cause problems. Pockets of tribesmen ventured out to steal horses. In inimitable fashion, Johnston came up with a plan to solve the situation. The following report was taken from the Billings Gazette (October 13, 1885):

> "Liver Eating Johnson, paying visit to Gazette office, gives his proposal to put stop to Piegan raids. His plan is simple: Posting lookouts in various sections of the country where Piegans travel, lookout to warn armed posses when Piegans appear, then capture Piegans and make them 'good Indians' out of all but one, sending the lone survivor with his hair cut off back to his tribe to report the treatment given his comrades. 'Really,' says Mr. Johnson, 'the only way to make a Piegan quit horse stealing is to kill him. That's my plan.'" (124)

Bear Hunting in 1885 with Madam de More

September 1885 finds Johnston still active, as he was scheduled to accompany Vic Smith on a hunting trip to Wyoming with French nobility, the Marquis and Madam de More. The Marquis's birth moniker was Antonio Mana de Vallambrosa, Marquis de More. He was no pilgrim. He attended the equivalent of West Point while a young man in France. The hunting party was going to meet Johnston at the Greybull River, in Wyoming, but due to mountain fever, Johnston was unable to accompany the group. (125)

Johnston is now sixty-one years of age. He is perhaps one year removed from his adventure in Hardwick's Wild West Show. The beaver season is two months away, and Johnston and Vic Smith will continue their wolfing endeavors. Since the buffalo were essentially exterminated by 1883, Johnston could no longer depend on buffalo hides as a source of income.

Threat of Crow Indian Uprising - October 1887

Since no information could be located as the where-abouts or activities of Johnston in 1886 (we can assume he continued hunting and perhaps guiding hunting trips into the mountains much like Vic Smith did), we move on to 1887.

The town of Billings was surprised to learn that some Crow Indians were creating problems in the area. No mention was made as to the nature of the problem, however. Following is the report recorded in Myrtle Cooper's book:

"The town (Billings) was on alert when it was informed that Sword Bearer and his followers surrendered." (126)

Interestingly, this "up-rising" brought Johnston and "Uncle" Billy Hamilton to the town of Billings due to Indian restlessness on the Crow Reservation led by a so-called medicine man, Sword Bearer, and 200 followers, intent on leading an Indian raid on the Billings community. The old Indian fighters "Liver-Eating" Johnson and "Uncle Billy Hamilton" came to town with their rifles ready and eager to protect the citizens and enter the battle. Soldiers from Fort Custer were on the alert, but a month later Sword Bearer was killed by an Indian near Billings. It can be assumed that Johnston and Hamilton lived in close proximity to Billings because they were apparently able to reach Billings in a short period to time.

This is further proof that Johnston was not a lawman in Billings in 1887 because Cooper stated that "Liver Eating Johnston and Uncle Billy Hamilton came to town....," thus inferring that Johnston was no longer a resident of Billings. In actuality, Johnston was living on a small island on the Yellowstone River at the time, within easy access to Billings.

Picture 39
Extreme Right- Crow Medicine Man Sword Bearer

Picture 40
"Sword Bearer" Makes the News
The Renowned Frontiersman,
"Uncle" Billy Hamilton

From Marshall to Cabbage Grower

Johnston left the Billings area and headed south. To the average citizen, Johnston must have seemed like a living artifact whose style of law enforcement was considered archaic and inappropriate for the "modern world."

After the excitement of the Crow Indian scare in October of 1887, Johnston can be found returning again to his solitary life. He was now sixty-three years of age. His health began to fail him. He began feeling increasing amounts of pain from his rheumatism for his many years of living on the plains and trapping in the cold waters of Montana's streams.

In addition, the gunshot wound sustained to his shoulder during the Civil War began to cause him grave problems. Johnston also had developed a medical condition called "erysipelas," which was an acute disease of the skin and tissues, causing many problems with lesions on his head, and creating painful inflammation. A notation in Johnston's "Declaration an Increase of an Invalid Pension" (April 10, 1889), details the recording physician's comments regarding Johnston's illness:

> "Increasing disability from said wound (Civil War gunshot wound to left shoulder during the battle of Newtonia) which produces soreness of the bone and breaking out... and withering away of said arm greatly disabling him for performance of manual labor." (127)

As sheriff, Johnston also had to deal with the effects of two gunshot wounds received in his right leg during various Indian fights, as well as "loss of sight of right eye... while an Indian Scout, under Generals Howard, Sturgis, Miles." (128)

In addition, he had to function with a "partial loss of hearing... caused by noise cannonry and exposure." (129) It was a true testament of his strength and endurance that he was able to function as well as he did for so many years.

Liver-Eating Johnston began receiving a small military pension of $4.00 per month beginning on June 18, 1884. This was a terribly inadequate sum of money that Johnston received in compensation for his meritorious service to his country during the Civil and Indian Wars. His pension eventually soared to $12.00 per month just before he died in January of 1900.

When Johnston left the town of Billings to live on a small island in the Yellowstone River, he craved isolation, wanting to be left alone to raise his cabbages. His goal was to take his ripe cabbages to Billings in hopes of making a little additional income for himself.

But when Johnston discovered that the going rate for cabbages was only three cents a pound, he said:

> "Three cents a pound? I sweated over them... cabbages all summer and I brought a load to town (Billings) and tried to sell them... think of me sweating over those... cabbages all summer long for three cents a pound. I'll go build me a cabin in the mountains where I can kill all I want to eat, and I'll never work again." (130)

True to his word, Johnston packed up his gear and headed southwest down the Yellowstone River toward Red Lodge, settling three miles from the growing community.

Johnston Builds a Cabin

Deciding to homestead on Rock Creek, Johnston built a small cabin with approximate dimensions of 15' x 20'. It was located about three miles south of the town of Red Lodge, Montana Territory. Buffalo Bill Cody used to pass by Johnston's cabin in order to reach his own ranch in present day Cody, Wyoming.

Johnston claimed one hundred sixty acres on the N1/4; NW1/4; SW1/4; NW1/4 and NW1/4; SW1/4, Section 9, Township 8 South, Range 20 East. (198)

Settling In At Red Lodge

Liver-Eating Johnston made many friends in his new community. He had mellowed somewhat in old age by the time he reached Red Lodge, and was able to develop many close friendships. His awesome reputation as an Indian fighter was, of course, quite well known to everyone in the entire territory.

The village of Red Lodge was founded in 1887 with the development of the Rocky Fork coal mine. It supplied coal for the Northern Pacific Railroad. As the town began to grow, there became a need to hire a sheriff, and Johnston was asked to take on the job. Despite his physical problems and his age, (64) he decided to accept the position, and became the first constable of the new town of Red Lodge.

Constable Johnston Begin His New Duties

Now that Johnston was an officer of the law again, he reverted back to the only way he knew how to keep the peace. He either kicked lawbreakers in the pants or banged their heads together. There was no jail, only a little one room log building, 10' x 12', which Johnston rarely used to house troublemakers.

The new Red Lodge constable purportedly never carried a gun in Red Lodge. A well-known studio photograph taken in Red Lodge in 1889 shows Johnston posed with a Winchester rifle and wearing a revolver or "short arm" as Johnston called it. But in reality, it was said that Johnston walked the streets of Red Lodge carrying no weapons.

A story written by Liver-Eating Johnston's good friend, Ben Greenough, details a typical method used by Johnston to keep the peace in Red Lodge.

"Liver-Eating Johnson was one of the strongest men I ever saw. He was over six feet tall, weighed 220 pounds, wore size 12 shoes. I remember one time, I was in an old saloon (George Howard's) near where

Red Lodge high school is now. I was playing Pin Pool with an old timer called Jack the Ripper. There was two little old Scotch miners, drunk and fighting on the floor. Johnston happened to pass by, looked in and saw them. He came in and picked them both off the floor, one under each arm. There was only plank sidewalks and a hitch pole, where they tied their saddled horses and teams in front of saloons and stores. Johnston walked out with those two men under his arms, fighting and cussing, laid them across the hitch post, banged their heads together, dropped them both down in the dirt, walked off and left they lying there. I thought he had killed them. They laid there for a few moments, then both got up and put their arms around each other – fight all out of them both, sober by that time." (131)

A Display of Johnston's Prodigious Strength

Other fascinating stories attesting to the raw strength of Liver-Eating Johnston were recorded by his good friend "Packsaddle" Ben Greenough (it was Johnston who so christened Greenough with the name Packsaddle).

The story goes that Greenough had been hard at work one-day digging fence post-holes for a rancher named John Henry. Greenough did not realize that Johnston was living at Henry's ranch. The following story depicts what happened one spring day in the early 1890's:

"In the early part of May, Johnson left to go hunt-ing on Cold Creek. About four or five o'clock one evening, "Pack Saddle" Ben glanced up the creek and saw an animal coming through the willows, only its enormous head could be seen, and Mr. Greenough, doing what anyone else would do un-der the circumstances, ran home to tell his em-ployer, who immediately came out with Ben. The object was clearly in view. It was Johnson carrying a 250-pound bear slung around his neck with its feet dangling." (132)

Carrying a 250 bear, wrapped around one's neck, is an incredible feat of strength for anyone. Johnston was probably around 70 when he purportedly performed this incredible stunt. One can easily surmise that in order to maintain his activity level, especially during his days as Indian fighter, hunter and trapper, Johnston had to consume large amounts of food in order to fuel his huge body.

Johnston Cracks Wise at Buffalo Bill Cody

Another interesting story by Harry Owens details Johnston's meeting up with Buffalo Bill Cody when Cody stopped at Red Lodge. Buffalo Bill was a passenger on the Meetesee Stage when it stopped at the Pollard Hotel in Red Lodge. The story tells us that Buffalo Bill stepped from the stagecoach wearing some fancy clothing. Johnston happened to spot him and walked over to greet him.

Johnston slapped Cody on the back, knocking his hat from his head. Liver-Eating then reportedly said "Buffalo Bill...the famous Indian fighter. The only Indian you ever put your hands on was a squaw!" Cody found Johnston's comment humorous and invited Johnston into the hotel to buy him a drink.

Johnston was not fond of Cody. However, there is great irony related to Johnston's disdain of Cody in that Johnston's body was exhumed and then re-interred from California in 1974 to a nearby town where Buffalo Bill made him home – Cody, Wyoming.

Picture 41
William F. Cody, a.k.a. Buffalo Bill

An Amusing Look at Johnston's Appetite

While Johnston served as Constable at Red Lodge, he was a frequent guest for dinner at the homes of Red Lodge citizens. One occasion stands out, as was reported by Johnston friend, Brownie Newton:

> "One day the Newtons and Johnson came to have dinner at the home of a mutual friend at Red Lodge. The lady of the house liked to make miniature biscuits that she built up on the plate until they came to a peak. She set the biscuits out on the table where the men were chatting and then returned to the kitchen to carry in the rest of the meal. 'Liver-eating began eating the biscuits by the handful, and when the hostess asked about them he said, 'Aw, heck, I thought them were crackers.'" (133)

One of Johnston's Last Act as Constable

One of the last recorded Red Lodge law enforcement activity involving Johnston occurred on June 21, 1894. The incident about Johnston was re-printed in Red Lodge's Carbon County News entitled "Tales of the First 100 years." In 1894 Johnston was 69 years of age, about to turn 70 in July. He was apparently still healthy enough to move around, as will be observed in the following narrative: Red Lodge: Constable saves murderers life:

June 21, 1894

> "One of Red Lodge's early murders occurred at the hour of 1:30 a.m. on June 19, 1894. The dastardly act took place in Martin Johnson's saloon. Patrick Cannon, an unmarried man, was shot down and killed by Frank Leadoff. The bullet entered his left eye and he died instantly. An angry mob gathered and it was feared that a necktie party was about to take place. Constable John Johnston was very

177

clever, however. He hustled Leadoff to the outskirts of town where he herded him around until morning and the passion of the populace had cooled down. Leadoff, who was married and the father of three little babies, the youngest only four weeks old, waived examination and was taken to Livingston, the County Seat, by Constable Johnston. Full circumstances of the case and the incident which led to the ultimate act were not known at that time, but it was expected that the slayer would plead self-defense." (134)

1895-Liver-Eating Johnston Visits Tombstone, Arizona

It is amazing to consider that Liver-Eating Johnston, at age seventy-one, felt strong enough to make a trip to visit the town Wyatt Earp made famous - Tombstone, Arizona. One wonders where Johnston was ultimately traveling when he made a detour in Tombstone. The following newspaper notation was printed in the November 1895 issue of the Tombstone Prospector and uncovered by my brother, Gary McLelland (owner of oldwesthistory.net).

"John Johnson, known as "Liver-Eating Johnson," the noted scout and Indian fighter, and irrepressible narrator of early day reminiscences, was in town today." (135)

This was probably the last of Johnston's adventures. His health began to falter in the mid 1890's, and it is reasonable to conclude that Johnston decided to take a final trip before his health deteriorated even more.

A
LIVER-EATING JOHNSTON
FACTOID

WILLIAM "BUFFALO BILL" CODY:
HALF REAL – HALF IMAGINED ?

"Buffalo Bill" essentially invented the Wild West show. However, frontiersmen knew that Cody and his public relations team "embellished" his frontier exploits. However, no one could ever deny the impact he and his troupe had upon all who witnessed his performances.

10

Crossing the Great Divide

The Death of John (Garrison) Johnston
January 21, 1900

The proud pioneer of the western plains could go no further. The Avenging Fury of the Plains was spent. His time had come. He had spent seven years as constable at Red Lodge and quickly began to deteriorate physically after 1895.

The ravages of time and the profound effect of battle wounds, as well as his rigorous mountain man experiences, all helped to take their toll, seemingly all at once, in late 1895.

Liver-Eating Johnston, bent over with rheumatism and spinal scoliosis, also felt the effects of a persistent skin disease, heart disease, a loss of vision in one eye, a general loss in hearing, and the rapid diminishing of his mobility.

To ease his pains, Johnston occasionally stayed at a local hot springs resort area where he hoped to gain relief for his tired, aching body.

However, when Johnston decided to leave the springs and return to Red Lodge, he spent more time in town than in his cabin. While in Red Lodge, he stayed with friends who took care of him. Being penniless (except for a small $12.00 military pension), Johnston had to rely on the good will of friends and neighbors. Johnston was a proud man, and hated to depend on charity; but he no other choice.

Johnston's physical problems had a positive side to them. Because he lived in Red Lodge most of the time, his cabin at Rock Creek was vacant. An interesting story about Johnston's generosity to an emigrant family during 1896 is presented below. A man wrote an article in 1990 that told about his mother being born in Johnston's cabin in the winter of 1896. Following is the story of Johnston's kindness to a family during the winter of 1896:

> "In 1896, two families set out from Council Bluffs, Iowa, in covered wagons to make their way to Red Lodge, Montana. One family was my grandparents, Mr. & Mrs. William Cunningham. The other was the Frank Linn family. On the way their cow died, so my Aunt Eva was fed on gruel made from oatmeal and water. When they arrived at Red Lodge they had one dollar between the two families. With this they bought a sack of flower. They had to live in the covered wagons, but with winter coming on, and my grandmother expecting a baby in March, they had to find shelter. "Liver-Eating" Johnson was living in town and not using his cabin up Rock Creek, so he offered it to my grandfather. In this cabin my Aunt Edna was born and two years later, my mother Bertha, came into the world. To "Liver-Eating" Johnson I owe much because if he had not offered his cabin for my aunt and mother to be born in, I may never have seen the light of day here in Red Lodge. This is the same cabin that has been restored to the museum along the highway today."
> (136)

The Slow Death of Liver-Eating Johnston

Johnston had become a prisoner, with only an attendant to meet his needs. His still powerful spirit was now confined to a rapidly decaying, broken down, body. He spent most of his time immobile.

Townspeople and reporters would come to visit. In all probability, many people wanted to have one final look at a genuine old west frontiersman, before he was forever gone. Johnston was in pain, and could not lie down in bed to sleep. He had to be propped up in chair in order to get some rest.

LIVER EATER' JOHNSON, NOTED INDIAN FIGHTER, SLEEPS IN LOS ANGELES CEMETERY

Picture 42
Johnston's Obituary Picture
His face tells a thousand stories.

For Johnston, life must have been a living hell. Memories of his past glories undoubtedly raced across the screen of his mind, reminding him of his once fearsome and unmatched physical skills and woodsman crafts.

He was alone. He had no family in Red Lodge; no wife, no children, no brothers or sisters. He had a sister living in Dover, New Jersey, when he died, and perhaps another sister also, but it is not known if Johnston corresponded with any of them. However, Johnston at least knew that one of his sisters, Matilda Tillman, was living in Dover, New Jersey, at the time of his death.

Despite what some Johnston researchers' state, Johnston could indeed read and write and, in all probability, did write to his sister nearly two thousand miles away. How would he have known he had a sister in Dover, New Jersey, if there was no correspondence between them?

Johnston's mind probably took him back to his boyhood days in Little York, New Jersey. He no doubt was reminded of his extremely difficult childhood, being "farmed out," to work for local farmers to pay his father's bills, according to Johnston researcher Dorman Nelson.

One also wonders if remembrances of his mother and family flashed across his mind, and if he regretted not seeing them since he left New Jersey.

Did he recall the pure thrill of seeing, for the first time, the massive whales that he signed on board to hunt? Did he regret striking the lieutenant on board ship during the Mexican War and then deserting? These rhetorical questions are fascinating to ponder, yet prove to be frustrating in that they will never be answered.

One can be certain that Johnston reviewed the many experiences of his amazing life. But did he have remorse at the wanton killing of hundreds of human beings during his wilderness experience? As tantalizing as the answers to these questions would be, they too are forever buried with Johnston in his final resting-place – Old Trail Town, Wyoming.

Johnston's final pension claim (November 15, 1899), details the terrible physical condition of Johnston's body:

"A progressive spinal scoliosis causes loss of power in limbs to the extent that he is unable to arise or lie down and requires the aid of attendant day and night. Also, arterial sclerosis and disease of the heart, and swelling of extremities. The disability is permanent." (137)

Shortly after filing his last claim to secure an increase in his pension, an article appeared in a local newspaper detailing Johnston's physical condition:

Yellowstone Journal

"One of the most famous characters of eastern Montana and the hero of many hairbreadth escapes during the days of Indian warfare on the northwestern frontier, is about to leave the scenes of his exploits forever. Liver-Eating Johnson has at last been compelled to yield to advancing age and cumulative effects of his years of exposure and hardship, and seeks rest and care in the national soldiers home in California, entrance to which he gained by various service in the Army. For weeks the old scout and Indian fighter has been bedridden at his home near Red Lodge and being without means has made application for admission to the home. The county in which he resides has agreed to defray the expenses of the trip and has also furnished an attendant. Gradually the ranks of the men who was the advance guard of civilization of the erstwhile wilderness and desert, which marked the boundary of what has grown into a prosperous and grand state are thinning and soon only their names will remain to be recalled by the story teller and the historian." (138)

Two weeks after this article was published, another article about Johnston appeared in the Carbon County Democrat. The article told of Johnston's departure on December 9, 1899, to California:

"John (Liver-Eating) Johnson departed Saturday for California, where he has permission to enter the soldiers' home. The health of the old scout has been failing very sadly for the past year, and his once powerful physique is not recognizable now in the feeble and broken-down old man, who boarded Saturday's train. Yet there was a time when the name of Liver-Eating Johnson was a terror to the Montana Indians, many of whom his trusty rifle had assisted in their search for a land where snow is at a premium. It was chiefly as a raconteur of the brave deeds of the past that the present generation knows the Liver-Eater, and his reminiscences were told with becoming modesty. From the commencement of this town, Johnson has made his home here. And it was plain to see that he was most reluctant to leave it, even when his better judgment convinced him against his will that it was the best part of wisdom to accept the provision made for the nation's heroes. Indeed, it is not a two-to-one bet that Dad Johnson will not turn around in his tracks, and come back to Red Lodge, to spend his few remaining days among the friends he loves and it would not be an unwelcome sight for a good many of our best citizens to see old Liver-Eater arrive at the Red Lodge station." (139)

Liver-Eating Johnston was, indeed, reluctant to leave Red Lodge. It was reported that:

"The old man broke down and wept like a child as the train whirled him away from his friends. It is fair to presume that his last thoughts as he lay dying in a strange land by the side of the sea, were of those generous friends and scenes of former days. Liver-Eating Johnson was a man among men. Brave and loyal, he never shirked a duty, never betrayed a friend, never gave quarter to a foe." (140)

The Great Liver-Eater Crosses the Great Divide

Johnston died at the National Soldiers home on Sunday, January 21, 1900, approximately one month after he arrived. The Carbon County Democrat (February 2, 1900) stated that it was clear that "Dad Johnson died of a broken heart. He wanted to be buried at Red Lodge, but sometimes we do not have the choice of our final resting place."

Twenty-four hours after Johnston died, he was buried in a wool-lined redwood casket in the national cemetery in West Los Angeles, and given a simple government head-stone that read:

Jon. Johnston, Co. H, 2nd Colo. Cavalry

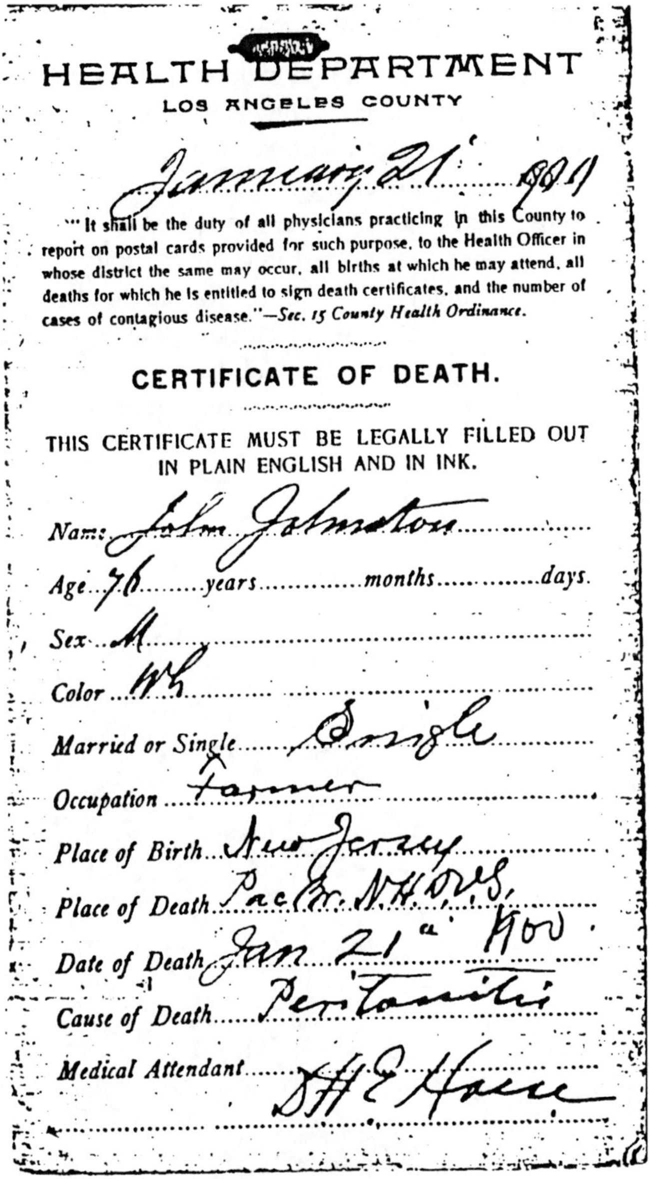

HEALTH DEPARTMENT
LOS ANGELES COUNTY

January 21 1911

"It shall be the duty of all physicians practicing in this County to report on postal cards provided for such purpose, to the Health Officer in whose district the same may occur, all births at which he may attend, all deaths for which he is entitled to sign death certificates, and the number of cases of contagious disease."—*Sec. 15 County Health Ordinance.*

CERTIFICATE OF DEATH.

THIS CERTIFICATE MUST BE LEGALLY FILLED OUT
IN PLAIN ENGLISH AND IN INK.

Name: *John Johnston*

Age *76* years months days

Sex *M*

Color *Wh*

Married or Single *Single*

Occupation *Farmer*

Place of Birth *New Jersey*

Place of Death *Pac. Br. N.H.D.V.S.*

Date of Death *Jan 21ª 1911*

Cause of Death *Peritonitis*

Medical Attendant *H. E. Hace*

Picture 43
Johnston's Death Certificate, Veterans Hospital
Los Angeles, CA.
Official cause of death – Peritonitis.

Johnston's Burial Upon Death

Prior to the exhumation and eventual removal of Johnston's body to a place called Old Trail Town, near Cody, Wyoming in 1974, Johnston's grave was only a few hundred feet from the busy and smoggy San Diego Freeway - hardly a fitting-resting place for Liver-Eating Johnston.

Johnston's body was placed into his shabbily made redwood casket on January 22, 1900. It would lie undisturbed for three quarters of a century until a group of 7th grade students from California decided that the true resting place of the famous pioneer belonged near the mountains that he loved so dearly.

Picture 44
The Great Rocky Mountains

A
LIVER-EATING JOHNSTON

FACTOID

DEATH CAME QUICKLY

Liver-Eating Johnston left Red Lodge, Montana, in December 1899 to enter the Veterans Hospital in California. His health had deteriorated to the point that his death was imminent. He died alone on January 21, 1900, hundreds of miles from the friends and mountains he loved so much.

11

Returning To Wyoming

In December of 1973, a group of 25 junior high school students from the Park View School in Lancaster, California felt that Liver-Eating Johnson's body didn't belong in a cemetery located directly in the middle of a large, urban city.

To Tri Robinson, their teacher and mentor, the Liver-Eater had been a hero of sorts, so much so that Robinson made Johnston the subject of his Master's degree thesis.

Robinson thought so highly of Johnston's role in the opening of the west that he spent one week in class discussing Johnston's life and legend with his 25 students. By the end of the week, both Robinson and his students felt that Johnston's remains belonged back in the plains of the Yellowstone basin, in either Montana or Wyoming.

Greatly moved by their lesson on Johnston, the students began a letter writing campaign to see if they could get Liver-Eating Johnston's bones "dug up" and shipped back to the land he loved so much. The idea evolved from a project that Robinson gave his students, the objective of which was learning how to write business letters,

Calling themselves the "Committee for Reburial of Liver-Eating Johnston," the students had written more than a dozen letters to governors, state and local historical societies, schools, and people of both influence and affluence in both Montana and Wyoming, in an attempt to garner support for their project.

During the months following their letter writing campaign, a man named Bob Edgar, the founder of Old Trail Town, near Cody, Wyoming, offered a final resting-place for Johnston. The students needed about $1000.00 for re-internment expenses. If they came up with the money, Johnston could be buried in Old Trail Town, Wyoming

Picture 45
Bob Edgar
"What Wisdom Is There Greater Than Kindness"
Jean-Jacques Rousseau

All Liver-Eating Johnston fans are grateful to Bob Edgar for permitting Johnston's remains to rest in hallowed ground in Cody, Wyoming.

Edgar's pioneer town is only forty-five miles south of Red Lodge. It was located in the heart of the land where Johnston roamed for much of his life. From Old Trail Town could be seen the Shoshone Canyon, the Beartooth Mountains, and Buffalo Heart Mountain, which Crow holy men ascended to seek visions from their spirit world. All of these sites were known and loved by Johnston, and Old Trail Town would indeed be a fitting location for Johnston's final home.

Seeking the Approval of the Veterans Administration

All of the efforts made by the students would have been in vain had they not received a favorable response from the Veterans Administration. Students wrote to an official by the name of Theodore Nix, superintendent of the national cemetery in Los Angeles, asking permission to remove Johnston's body and bring it to Old Trail Town, Wyoming, for re-internment. The letter stated that:

> "... it is documented that he (Johnston) wished to be buried in the Big Sky country. It is our aim to fulfill his earlier request. Johnston should be transferred back to the country where he put his mark on history." (141)

The students received a reply, which stated there were no relatives who could officially, and legally, request a relocation of Johnston's remains. At that time, the Veterans Administration apparently had no idea that Mrs. M. Tillman, of Dover, New Jersey, was indeed a relative - Johnston's sister.

The next step was to contact Washington, D.C., and attempt to solicit their approval. But the students found out that the government usually considers internment final, especially when the graves are as old as Johnston's was.

Weeks passed without a final decision from the Veterans Administration headquarters in Washington, D.C. But then, on May 14, 1974, Robinson received a phone call from Washington, stating that the decision was imminent. A few days later, Mr. Rufus Wilson, Director of the National Cemetery system, had informed Superintendent Nix that disinterment and removal had been approved. But one major problem remained.

Bypassing the Next of Kin Law

There exists a law that states emphatically that only a relative, or "next of kin," can authorize the removal of a relative's remains. Apparently Johnston's family in New Jersey knew nothing about Johnston's death, or else perhaps they may have made special arrangements to ship their brother's body back to New Jersey for burial.

Since no relatives came forward, Robinson's committee was declared, in an unprecedented maneuver, to be the next-of-kin and was given the legal authority to move Johnston's remains. (142)

With the promises of Edgar's financial support already secured, exhumation took place on June 4, 1974.

Trouble from Red Lodge

The citizens of Red Lodge, Montana, had previously made no attempt to secure the body of their former constable. No previous effort was made to claim the body for a final resting place within the borders of the town where he spent the last twelve years of his life.

A Red Lodge newspaper reporter named Dave Henderson, a staff writer on the Carbon County newspaper, spearheaded the rationalization for this inaction. Henderson felt that there should be no fanfare about Johnston's final burial place. He stated that:

"the entire project borders on making a hero out of someone who was just an Indian fighter, and apparently the idea hasn't been that well received in Red Lodge. There's no doubt he was a colorful figure in American history, but I think there are still mixed feelings here where so many Indians still live." (143)

But when it was known that Johnston was to be buried in nearby Cody, Wyoming, Congressional Representative John Melcher, acting on behalf of the town of Red Lodge, convinced the Director of the National Cemeteries to stop the exhumation because he felt Johnston's remains should, after all, be placed in the city where he last lived and worked – Red Lodge, Montana.

Robinson and his students waited anxiously for what would be the next action taken in the dizzying saga regarding the fate of Liver-Eating Johnston's remains. Then, finally, to the great joy of Robinson and his students, the Director relented after being bombarded with phone calls and protesters who supported the students' efforts. The exhumation was to proceed as scheduled.

Opening Johnson's Grave

It was hoped that the exhumation of Johnston's remains was going to be conducted with dignity and grace. However, this hope was overshadowed by weeks of media hype and political in fighting. As the cemetery workers stood graveside, ready to remove the soil that had enveloped Johnston's redwood casket for three-quarters of a century, an NBC mobile van appeared, replete with reporters.

A Graveside "Circus"

Helicopters buzzed overhead, hoping to film the event from the air. In order to gain a bit of privacy, Cemetery Superintendent Nix erected a canvas canopy over to Johnston's gravesite to shield his memory from further indignity.

Surrounding the gravesite were Robinson and his students. The air was thick with excitement and anticipation, and the students nervously waited for the working crews to begin their task.

Within a few moments, cemetery workers began to remove, shovel by shovel, the soil that covered Johnston's coffin for so long. Foot by foot they invaded this long ignored resting-place, stopping only to alert Superintendent Nix that they had finally reached Johnston's remains.

Only A Leg Bone (Or Two)

The curious onlookers must have been greatly disappointed when the workers reached Johnston's remains. Would they see a semblance of what the famed pioneer looked like? Would they see his clothing? Was he buried with any personal belongings?

When the workers reached Johnston's remains, they discovered that the flimsy coffin in which Johnston was buried had disintegrated. All that remained of the once powerful and fearful Indian fighter were small pieces of the Liver-Eater's coffin, a thighbone (some reports state that there were two thighbones), a few of Johnston's teeth, a few metal buttons and rusted casket handles.

Johnston's remains were reverently gathered, along with his original headstone, and placed into a temporary plywood coffin in preparation for shipment to Cody, Wyoming.

A Threat of Body-Snatching

Unbelievably, Robinson had to take precautions against a possible body-snatching attempt of Johnston's coffin. This was arranged because of a phone call by someone from Red Lodge seeking information about the scheduled shipment of Liver-Eating Johnston's body to the Cody area.

With Johnston's coffin lying securely in a mortuary van, Robinson arranged for a protective convoy to follow closely behind the funeral wagon. The van made its way through the back streets of Santa Monica, drove along the San Diego Freeway, and went directly to the freight offices at Los Angeles airport, where a plane from Western Airlines had offered to transport the coffin to Wyoming.

Robinson and a six-student committee followed in another plane, the tickets provided again by Western Airlines.

When Johnston's coffin reached Casper, Wyoming, Bob Edgar secured it and transported it to Cody. Robinson and his students arrived a short time later, breathing collective sighs of relief that their goal of re-internment of Johnston's remains would soon be realized.

Picture 46
Crow Killer Author-Robert Bunker
In this 1950's photo, Bunker kneels at Johnston's gravesite
at the Veterans Cemetery in Los Angeles, California

A
LIVER-EATING JOHNSTON
FACTOID

OLD TRAIL TOWN -
JOHNSTON'S FINAL RESTING PLACE

Owned by Bob Edgar, Old Trail Town is a collection of 26 historic buildings in Cody, Wyoming. Featured along with the gravesite of Johnston is the "Hole in the Wall" gang's cabin of Butch Cassidy and the Sundance Kid. The site also honors the famed Custer Crow scout, Curly, and Custer himself.

12

A Monument of Honor

The newspapers stated that there were approximately 1,200 onlookers in Old Trail Town on Saturday, June 8, 1974, to honor the memory of Johnston as his remains were lowered by rope in a carved out 3' x 9' burial plot which had been only recently prepared.

Liver-Eating Johnston was laid to rest on a grassy hill just outside of Old Trail Town that boasted a clear view of his beloved Absaroka Mountains. The threatening thunderheads had finally dissolved, replaced by a bright Montana sun that burst through the clouds as if saluting the misty memory of the Liver-Eater.

Robert "Jeremiah Johnson" Redford Arrives

Among the 1,200 people who gathered to honor Johnston was actor Robert Redford. Since Redford portrayed Jeremiah Johnson in the 1970's hit movie of the same name, he gladly accepted the invitation to serve as chief pallbearer and deliverer of a brief eulogy about Johnston's impact upon the opening of the west.

In a supposed "coincidence," the Warner Brothers' Motion Picture studio had been massively promoting the movie "Jeremiah Johnson" during the same months that Robinson and his students were making plans to bring Johnston's remains back to Wyoming.

They even provided film clips from Redford's movie to the various television networks covering the re-internment. The entire nation thus had an opportunity to learn who Jeremiah Johnson was, although the representation they witnessed was completely erroneous.

Nationally known columnist Jack Anderson became interested in the proceedings of Johnston's reburial. In an article written on June 19, 1974, Anderson was curious about the so-called "coincidence" between Johnston's burial and the release of Redford's movie.

Anderson wrote: "a spokesman for Warner Brothers denied that the moviemakers promoted Jeremiah Johnson's reburial, calling the event a 'fluky publicity break.' As for Robert Redford, he lives in the mountains and has a genuine interest in the mountain man he portrayed," (144)

A Step Back In Time

Among the gathering multitude of people was a troop of latter-day U.S. Cavalry horse soldiers, an American Legion honor guard, "mountain men" dressed in darkened buckskins like the pioneers of old, bearing rifles used to fire a volley for a final salute to the Liver-Eater. There was also a bugler in attendance, blowing both "taps" and the Battle Hymn of the Republic, both of which greatly added to the emotion of the ceremony.

Redford's Speech

To his credit, Robert Redford didn't want his "celebrity status" to upstage the ceremony for Liver-Eating Johnston's reburial. He had reportedly, and emphatically, informed the Warner Brothers' publicity agent that the focus belongs on the 7th grade class from California, and not his appearance at the ceremony.

Redford flew into Cody via a Lear jet early Saturday morning on June 8th with his son, Jamie. Prior to the scheduled start of the ceremony at 1:00 PM, Redford had time to sit quietly to write and memorize the comments about Johnston that he was soon to deliver.

When it was time to deliver his message, Redford stepped to the public address podium. He was warmly greeted by the audience and fans. Following are the remarks made by Redford:

> "I am grateful to the students of the seventh grade class of Lancaster, California, who showed the same kind of enterprise and spirit that characterized early figures like Jeremiah Johnson. In the current climate of natural events, we could all learn from them. I am honored and grateful to be here." (145)

Additional remarks were recorded on that June 8th afternoon by Redford that further honored the efforts of Robinson and the 7th graders:

> "We do films for a lot of reasons, and hope for many satisfactions. In Jeremiah Johnson we tried, through the character, to illuminate the joys, hardships, and sorrows of life in the wilderness. It was a very personal film for me and it is a moving experience for me to be here today and see the qualities we tried to portray in the film present in the endeavors of these young people and their teacher. It is rewarding to see such an earnest concern for the protection of our historical characters. It is a concern I share. In light of current events, we may have to look back in time a bit to see where to go from here. These young people are responsible for this and I am grateful. With the energy and ideas displayed by these young people, they just might take over the world. And that wouldn't be such a bad idea." (146)

Why The Movie Was Called "Jeremiah Johnson"

Liver-Eating Johnston's real name was John Johnston (a.k.a. John Garrison). But film director Sidney Pollack preferred to use the fictitious name, Jeremiah Johnson. With the freedom to manipulate film scripts and ignore history, the world received another Hollywood "treat," that ran counter to reality.

Director Sidney Pollack's rationalization for not using Johnston's correct name is given below. Pollack said he chose the name Jeremiah because:

> "We wanted him to be an allegorical character, a symbol of all mountain men. We felt that we would give a wider interest to the film. I don't know if the next generation will take Jeremiah for the real name or not, but that's why we called our character Jeremiah instead of John. We wanted him to be a larger than life symbol of all such men." (147)

Interestingly, the original film script had a liver-eating sequence written into it. But Pollack cut it from the film when he couldn't technically handle the scene. Thankfully, it was not included in the movie because it would have only further confused the public about Johnston's true exploits.

Liver-Eater's Grave Is Sealed

It was decided that no opportunity would be given to any potential "body snatcher" who wanted to remove Johnston's remains. To ensure this, cement was poured over the pine coffin. Edgar wanted to take no chances in providing Johnston a final resting-place.

As the cement dried, Edgar placed a buffalo skull in the wet cement as one final tribute to the man whom Edgar unselfishly brought back to the mountains that Johnston so loved. Eventually, Johnston's burial site was enclosed with an iron grave fence; similar to the type used in cemeteries during the 1800's.

A red stone monument five feet high and four feet wide was placed on the grave, bearing a metal tablet that briefly described the impressive life of Liver-Eating Johnston.

The Red Lodge Fight Continued

Even though Johnston was buried in Old Trail Town, Wyoming, the town of Red Lodge still wanted Johnston's final home to be where he lived twelve years before his death in Red Lodge.

A Red Lodge organization called "Montana Friends of John J. Johnston" had their attorney file suit in the Federal District Court arguing the Veterans Administration's decision of allowing Johnston's body to be buried in Cody. The petition was filed one week after Liver-Eater was buried on June 8, 1974.

After a wait of six months, a hearing was scheduled during Christmas week of 1974 in the U.S. District Court in Billings, Montana, to discuss motions in a suit brought by the citizens of Red Lodge against the Veterans Administration and Rufus Wilson, the VA's assistant administrator of cemetery services.

The suit sought to exhume Johnston's remains and move them back to Red Lodge. Judge James Batten, of the Billings District of the U.S. Federal Court, was the presiding judge. After considerable deliberation, Judge Batten ruled that the attempt by the Red Lodge citizens to obtain a court order to move Johnston's coffin was "without merit." The judge then ordered a dismissal of the case.

Before the final decision was rendered, the late Harry Owens, the Johnston historian and leader of the Montana Friends of John J. Johnston, waxed philosophic about the final result of the judge's order. Owens felt that "even if the lawsuit fails, I believe that there are still many opportunities for increasing historical awareness in the Red Lodge area." (148)

So, finally, after a year of letter writing, politicking, maneuvering and waiting, the 7th grade kids from Park View Junior High School realized their dream. The compassionate concern for the memory of the long-forgotten frontiersman helped to provide an object lesson that they would never forget.

They were taught that dreams could, indeed, be realized, even for a bunch of 13-year old junior high school kids. They had learned that nothing is really impossible, that the passion of their teacher to "right a wrong" is something that simply cannot be taught in a classroom.

Ultimately, they realized that concern for the memory of Liver-Eating Johnston, regardless of their hero's flaws, is trans-generational. They discovered that love, duty and honor are not bound by time, but by the size of their hearts.

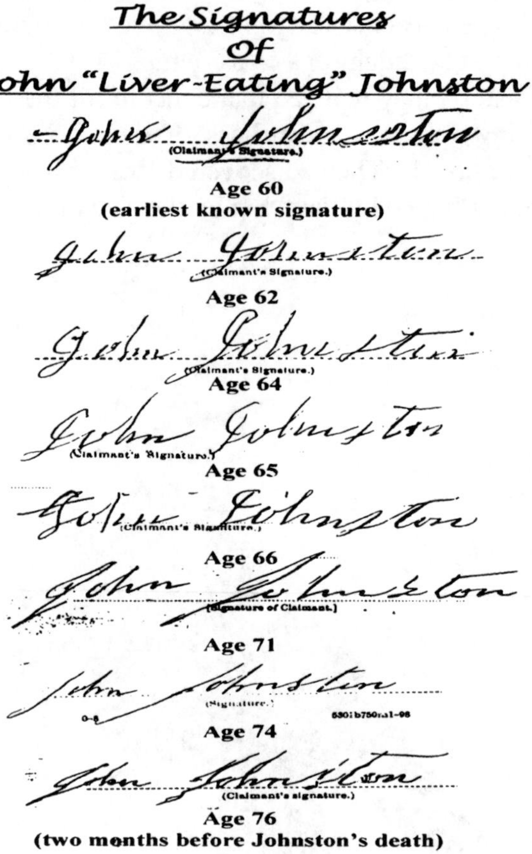

The Signatures
Of
John "Liver-Eating" Johnston

(Claimant's Signature.)

Age 60
(earliest known signature)

(Claimant's Signature.)

Age 62

(Claimant's Signature.)

Age 64

(Claimant's Signature.)

Age 65

(Claimant's Signature.)

Age 66

[Signature of Claimant.]

Age 71

(Signature.)

Age 74

(Claimant's signature.)

Age 76
(two months before Johnston's death)

Picture 47
Signatures secured from Johnston's
Military/ Pension Records

Picture 48
Liver-Eating Johnston's Last Trail
Old Trail Town, Cody, Wyoming

PHOTO CREDITS

Cover   Johnston at Fort Keogh - 1877
                 Yale University Press, 1926

Picture 2   Johnston in 1899
                 The Billings Gazette, 1912

Picture 3   Friends, Acquaintances & Enemies

John X Beidler
         Courtesy of Cowan's Auctions

Trophies
         Courtesy of Billings Public Library

Luther Sage Kelly
         Courtesy of USDA Forest Service

General Nelson A. Miles
         Courtesy of Library of Congress

Grant Marsh
         Courtesy of the National Park Service

Calamity Jane
         Courtesy of Library of Congress

General Samuel Sturgis
         Courtesy of Library of Congress

General James Blunt
         Courtesy of Library of Congress

Confederate General Sterling Price
         Courtesy of Library of Congress

Sioux Chief Sitting Bull
         Courtesy of Library of Congress

INDEX

A

Abolitionists, 58
"A History of Montana," 80,112
African Americans, (early west), 16-18,62
Alberta, Canada, 118
Alcohol (Johnston), 7,8,9, 117-122
Alcohol problem(s) (Miles' command), 132
Alder Gulch, Mon Territory, 38,40,46,49
Allen, "Doc,"William, 113-114
American Horse (Sioux Chief), 127
Anaconda Standard (newspaper), 92
Anderson, Jack (journalist), 198
Anderson, "White Eye," 5,
Anderson, William (Bloody Bill), 36,58
Arapaho Nation, 37
Ash Creek (battle of), 135
Assiniboin Nation, 141
Avenging Fury of the Plains (Johnston), 159,180

B

Bad Medicine (California gold miners), 32
Bad Medicine (Johnston known as), 2,75
Bailey, George (rode with Portugee Phillips), 11
Bannack (gold strike), 38-42
Bark Creek (battle of), 135
Batten, Judge James, 202
Baxter Springs, KS. (battle of), 60
Bear Claw, 5
Beaver, 34-35,167
Beaver Hats, 35
Beaver Pelts (plews), 35
Beidler, John "X", 3,5,11,29,42-43,74,76-77,83,
        117,151,161

C

Carson, Kit, xv
Carver, "Doc" W.F., 19
Cedar Creek (battle of), 135
Cherokee Nation, 9,62
Cherry Creek, Colo., (mining town), 36
Cheyenne Nation, xv, 134-135,142
Chief Joseph (Nez Perce), 2,105,136,140
Clendenning (Fort Hawley fight), 73,92
Cochrane, J.M.V., 142
Committee for the Reburial of Johnston, 190
Confederate Gulch (mining camp), 45,116
Cooper, Myrtle E., 167
Coulson-Billings Post (newspaper), 157
Coulson, Mont. Territory, 18,142,149-150
Coulson, S.B., 149
Coulson Steamboat(s), 149
Crazy Horse, 2,126,128
"Crimsoned Prairie: The Indian Wars," 4
Crook, General George 126-127
Crow Nation, xvi, 3,5,7,113,127
Crow Scouts, 103
Cushine, Tom (scout), 127
Custer County, Mont. Territory, 18

D

Daily Leader (newspaper), 105
Davis, President Jefferson, 44-46
Death Certificate (Johnston's), 187
Del Gue (fictional character), 5
De More, Marquis and Madame, 167-168
Dennis, Pomp, 94,116
Descriptive List of Deserters (Johnston), 58
"Desertion During the Civil War," 55-56
Desertion (Civil War), 10,56
Desertion (Mexican War), xvii, 25-26
Diamond R Freight Company (Johnston as teamster), 74
Dillon Examiner (newspaper), 99

Dorson, Richard, 2
Dover, New Jersey (home of Johnston's sister), 183
Dry Gulch, Colo, (mining town), 36

E

Earp, Morgan, 163
Edgar, Bob, 190-191
Edgerton, Sidney, 47

F

Far West (steamboat), 83,
Fendrich, Anne, 8
Fetterman, Capt. William J., 11,82
Fifth Cavalry, 126
Fifth Infantry, 128,131,140
Fifteenth Kansas, 61
Fire Devil (Sioux name for Johnston), 88
First Colorado Cavalry, 51
Fisk, Captain James, 47
Flathead Nation, xvi, 7
Fleury, George, (scout), 127
Ford, Brig. General James (Johnston commander), 61,65
Fort Benton, Montana Territory, 9,74,117,118
Fort Buford, 141
Fort Hawley, Montana Territory, 82
Fort Kearny, Wyo., 11
Fort Keogh, Mont., 140-141
Fort Laramie, Wyo., 11,35
Fort Leavenworth, Ks., 57,69
Fort Pease, 37,161
Fort Rice, 109
Fort Riley, 65
Fort Spitzee, (whiskey fort), 118
Fort Sumpter, NC., 57
Fort Whoop Up, 123
Fort Wise Treaty, 37

Forty Rod, (whiskey), 120
Fourth Missouri Infantry, 17

G

H

I

"I Buried Hickok," 5
Independence. Mo., (battle of), 63
Indian Wars of 1876-1877, xiv, 2
Innocents (Sheriff Plummer's band of cutthroats), 40
Iron Star (Cheyenne Chief), 144
Irvine, Tom (Johnston friend and employer), 18,151,156-
    157, 164

J

Jackson, Billy, (scout), 127
Jackson, Bob, (scout), 127
Jensen, Joyce, 20, 157-158
Johnson, Dorothy, 12
Johnson, George (Johnston friend), 127
Johnson, Jeremiah (Hollywood name for Johnston), 198
Johnston, John, (aka Garrison),
    earns name "liver-eating," xiii, 92-98; helped open
    West, xiv; gaps in timeline, xv; a.k.a., John Garrison,
    xv, xvii; joins Wild West show, xv, 19-20; in Mexican
    War, xvi, 5, 17, 24-25, 29; and Flathead wife, xvi, 3; de-
    serts Mexican War, xvi, 29-30; deserts Civil War, 10,
    25-26; born in Little York, N.J., xvii, 22; Spenser rifle
    of, xviii; feared by Indians, 1; known as bad medicine,
    2; military pension of, 3; in U.S. Navy, 3; came from
    Pacific coast, 3; partner of "X" Beidler,5; partner of Vic
    Smith, 5; myth of eating Crow livers, 5; as "cannibal,"
    6; suffered from rheumatism, 6; medical problems of, 6;
    and alcohol problems, 7-9; and scalping, 9; myth of Por-
    tugee Phillips, 11; myth of Mariano Modeno,13; and
    friend Muggins Taylor, 18; as Justice of the Peace, 18;
    and friendship with Tom Irvine, 18; height of, 21; had
    five sisters, 22; as whaler, 22-24; fought Indians in Cali-
    fornia, 32-33; as trapper, 34; as buffalo hunter, 34; and
    myth of eating Blackfoot Indian's leg, 41; and Rebels in
    mining camps, 44; Civil war wounds of, 57; mustered

out of Army, 69; military medical records of, 70; and events after Civil War, 73; as woodhawk, 73, 76-78; as teamster, 74; known as bad medicine, 75; profile of, 75; sells scalps, 80, 91; aboard steamship Nile, 83; eats ice cream for first time, 83; sets trap for Sioux, 85-86; poisons Sioux warriors with strychnine, 86; known as fire devil, 88; helps build bridge over Yellowstone, 89; and a Crow wife(?), 109; enters spitting contest, 113; gives up woodhawking, 117; as whiskey peddler, 117; taken advantage of, 121; as Army scout with Gen. Miles, 125; nearly killed, 135; in Nez Perce War of 1877, 136; as Yellowstone scout, 141; commended by General Hugh Scott, 144-145; as horse thief, 145; as sheriff, 147; runs a stagecoach business, 147; shoots at passenger on train, 153-154; and steamboat captain Grant Marsh, 149; as Justice of the Peace, 150; a.k.a., Jack Johnson, 150; as County Deputy, 151, known as strong man, 151, 173, 174; usually dressed in buckskins, 155; ate thirteen buffalo over winter, 155-156; appetite of, 155-156; made no arrests as sheriff of Coulson, 156-157; transports six prisoners, 157; and death of Muggins Taylor, 157-158; fights professional boxer, 162-163; and bogus photo, 163-165; loses sheriff's job at Coulson, 164; and Piegan raids, 167; and bear hunting, 167; involvement of 1887 Crow uprising, 167; as cabbage grower, 171; military pension of, 171-172; medical problems of, 171, builds a cabin, 172; moves to Red Lodge, 173; teases Buffalo Bill Cody, 175; and biscuit eating, 177; rescues murderer from lynch mob, 177-178; visits Tombstone, AZ., 178; death of, 182,186; saves a family, 181; at Hunter Hot Springs, 181; obituary of, 182; buried at Old Trail Town, Wyo., 185; death certificate of, 187; exhumation of, 193-194; and body snatching threat, 195; monument of, 201.

#

Kelly, Yellowstone (Luther S), 2, 128, 130, 131, 132-133, 136,146.
Koch, Peter, 80

L

Lame Deer (Cheyenne Chief), 144
Lane, Senator Joseph, 58
LeForge, Tom (scout with Johnston), 128
Lethbridge Daily Herald, 119
Lewis and Clark, 136
Lincoln, Abraham, 45-46
Little Blue, Mo, (battle of), 63
Little York, NJ (Johnston born in), 22,183
Longmore, Fred, 28
Lonn, Ellen, 56
Lumpp, Henry (murdered Muggins Taylor), 18, 158
Lyon, Captain Nathaniel, 57

M

Marsh, Cpt. Grant (steamboat pilot), 83, 85, 149
Marshall, S.L.A., 4
Marvin, Burt, 81
"Massacre: Tragedy at White River," 14
McAdow, P.W., (founded village of Coulson), 149
McGavin, John, 38
McGirl, Tom, 114-115
Medina, Mariano, 14-16
Melcher, Congressman John, 194
Merritt, Col. Wesley, 126
Mexican War, xvi, 5,17,24-25
Miles City, Mont., 18
Miles, General Nelson A., xiv, 2,100, 125,127-129,142
Minniconjou Sioux, 128
Missouri border ruffians (bushwhackers), 60
Modeno, Mariano (fictitious character), 13
Montana Friends of John Johnston, 202

BIBLIOGRAPHY

CHAPTER 1

1. Kelly, Luther S, 1926, Yellowstone Kelly: *The Memoirs of Luther S. Kelly*, Ed. By M.M. Quaife, Lincoln, Yale University Press, p. 167
2. Thorpe, Raymond W., & Bunker, Robert, *Crow Killer*: *The Saga of Liver-Eating Johnson*. Indiana University Press, Bloomington, 1958.
3. Ibid, p. 7
4. Ibid, p. 21
5. Declaration For The Increase Of An Invalid Pension, June 12, 1884, Minneapolis, Minn.
6. Rex Bundy, 11 March 1977. "Liver-Eating Johnston," Wild West Magazine.
7. Helen Fitzgerald Sanders, 1913-4 History of Montana (Chicago, The, Lewis Publishing Co.), p. 233
8. Will Carpenter, December 1971, "The Truth About Liver Eating Johnston." Westerner Magazine, p. 36.
9. S.L.A. Marshall, 1972, Crimsoned Prairie (New York. Scribner Book Company), p. 56.
10. Thorpe and Bunker, 1958, p. 22.
11. Ibid, p. 51.
12. Billings Times, July 27, 1899
13. The Pioneer Press, December 21, 1884, St. Paul, Minn.
14. Thorpe and Bunker, 1958. p. 64.
15. Eric Thane, 1942, High Border Country. (New York. Duell, Sloan, & Pearce), p. 69
16. Ann Fendrich. 25 January, 1967. "Liver Eating Johnson." The Park County Rustler.
17. R. M. Husbandman, 3 March. 1938. "Benton Crowd Jobbed Butter-In Using 'Liver-Eating' Johnston Stooge to Bad Competition. (Article Only – Unknown newspaper source).
18. Thorpe and Bunker, 1958, p. 90.

19. Thorpe and Bunker, 1958, p. 101.
20. Ibid. p. 101.
21. Jon E. Lewis, 1999, *The Mammoth Book of the West* (New York, Carroll & Graf Publishers), pgs. 378-379.
22. Bozeman Trail Association and Foundation - Fort Phil Kearny, 12 Dec. 1999.
23. Dorothy M. Johnson. 1971. *The Bloody Bozeman.* (New York, McGraw-Hill Book Company), p. 238.
24. Thorpe and Bunker, 1958, p. 147.
25. Marshall Sprague, 1957, *Massacre: The Tragedy at White River,* (Boston, Little, Brown & Company), pgs. 325-326.
26. Johnston never having seen a Negro is absurd. (Thorpe and Bunker. 1958, p. 157) It is incomprehensible that Thorpe and Bunker would have readers believe their claim. At Benton Barracks, where Johnston enlisted, there were the 1st, 2nd, 3rd, and 4th Missouri Colored Infantry units training alongside Johnston's 2nd Colorado Cavalry.
27. Paula Mitchell Marks, 1994, Precious Dust: The Saga of the Western Gold Rushes (Lincoln, University of Nebraska Press), p. 288
28. Brian Albrecht & Dave Davis, AfricanAmericans.com, (Accessed March 28, 6:00 pm)
29. 29. William Loren Katz, 1987, The Black West: A Documentary and Pictorial History of the African American Role in the Westward Expansion of the United States. (New York, Simon and Schuster), p. 115.
30. Thorpe and Bunker, p. 179
31. Myrtle E. Cooper, 1981, From Tent Town to City: A Chronological History of Billings, Montana 1882-1935 (Billings, Self – Published), p. 3.
32. Ibid. 1981, p. 8.
33. The whitewashed portrayal of Johnston by Thorpe and Bunker as the "noble savage" is evident in their writings. Johnston was willing to involve himself in any en-

terprise if there was money to be made. Thorpe and
Bunker, 1958, p. 187.
34. Joyce M. Jensen, p. 40. There are three accounts that
describe Johnston's involvement in the Hardwick Wild West
Show (circus). The late Harry Owens could not identify the
name of the show to which Johnston was attached and stated
that the show broke up in Iowa. Fellow scout Tom LeForge
stated that the show went bankrupt in St. Paul, Minnesota.
The Livingston newspaper account of August 16, 1884
contains the most accurate description.

CHAPTER 2

35. "How Liver-Eatin' Johnson Got His Uncouth Name,"
July 18, 1899, Anaconda Standard, p. 14.
36. Carbon County Democrat, February 7, 1900, p. 1.
37. Will Carpenter, Westerner Magazine, 1971, pgs. 36-37.
38. Harry B. Weiss, 1994, Whaling In New Jersey, New
Jersey Agricultural Society, Trenton, New Jersey, p. 40.
39. There has been occasional speculation that Johnston also
signed on with a British Man of War (see Billings Gazette,
1914- no date given) or on a merchant cargo ship. Military or
pension records have never verified these claims. Carbon
County Democrat, Feb. 7, 1900.
40. Ibid. p. 1.
41. Jack K. Bauer, 1974, *The Mexican War: 1846-1848,*
(Lincoln, University of Nebraska Press), p. 115.
42. Johnston died at the Pacific Branch of the Veterans
Hospital, Los Angeles, California on January 21, 1900 of
peritonitis at the age of 76 years, 5 months. He would remain
for the next 74 years until being exhumed and re-interred at
Trail Town, Wyoming. *Certificate of Death, Health Depart-
ment-* Los Angeles, California, January 21, 1900.
43. Elno, Helena Independent (article only -date and year of
specific publication unknown)
44. Rex Bundy, 1991, True West, p. 11
45. Helen F. Sanders, 1913, p. 233.

46. Joseph Lewis French, *The Pioneer West,* (New York, Indian Head Books), 1995, p. 88.

47. Liver Eating Johnson is Foully Slandered in the Pioneer Press," December 25, 1884, The Post of Billings and Yellowstone County, Mt., Vol. III, No. 45, p. 1.

48. J. P. Dunn Jr., 1886, Massacres of the Mountains: A History of the Indian Wars of the Far West–1815-1875 (New York, Archer House Inc.), P. 111.

49. Ibid. 1886, p. 111.

50. Ibid. p. 111.

CHAPTER 3

51. Jay Monaghan, 1955, Civil War on the Western Border: 1854-1865, (Lincoln, University of Nebraska Press), p. 275.

52. The Billings Gazette, November 10, 1940.

53. The Bynum Herald, March 27, 1922

54. Eric Thane, 1942, High Border Country, (New York, Duell, Sloan & Pearce), p. 91.

55. Edwin Ruthven Purple, 1995, ed., Kenneth N. Owens, Perilous Passage: A Narrative of the Montana Gold Rush, 1862-1863 (Helena, Montana Historical Society), pgs. 101-102.

CHAPTER 4

56. Lonn, Ella, 1998, p. vi.

57. Duane Schultz, 1996, Quantrill's War: The Life and Times of William Clarke Quantrill (New York, St Martin's Press), p. 134.

58. Ibid. 1996, p. 134.

59. Thomas Goodrich, 1995, Black Flag: Guerilla Warfare on the Western Border, 1861-1865 (Bloomington, Indiana University Press), p. 7.

60. Ibid. 1995, p. 133

61. Ibid. p. 133.

62. Jay Monaghan, 1955, p. 175.

63. Official Army Register of the Volunteer Force of the United State Army for the Years1861-1865. U.S. Government Printing Office, Washington, DC., July 16, 1867, p. 507.

64. Ibid. p. 507.

65. Department of the Interior, Record and Pension Office, Bureau of Pensions, Commissioner of Pensions, December 10, 1897

CHAPTER 5

66. The Independent Record, 30 January 1983, Helena, Montana, p. 4c.

67. "The Story of Liver-Eating Johnson," The Dillon Examiner (copy of article only -no date given).

68. Will Carpenter, 1971, p. 36.

69. Ibid. 1971, p. 62.

70. Johnston's frontier experiences were occasionally captured in local newspaper articles. He had developed a reputation as a man who was perhaps the elite among Indian fighters of his generation. *Billings Weekly Gazette*, January 24, 1889.

71. Helen F. Sanders, 1913, p. 234.

72. Eric Thane, 1942, p. 69.

73. L.W. Randall, 1961, Footprints Along the Yellowstone (San Antonio, The Naylor Company), p. 119.

74. E. Brinstool, 1953, Fighting Indian Warriors (New York: Indian Head Books), pgs. 36-37.

75. "Liver-Eating Johnson: The Noted Frontiersman Passes Away. February 7, 1900. The Carbon County Democrat, No. 11, p. 1.

76. "Experiences On the Upper Missouri in 1866," November 28, 1910, Montana Outlook, Vol. 2, No. 22.

77. "Liver-Eating Johnson: The Career of a Yellowstone County Man, As Pictured in a Leading Eastern Journal, 24 January 1889, Billings Weekly.

78. Anne Fendrich, Anne's Archives, The Cody Rustler, January 30, 1967, pg. 1

CHAPTER 6

79. Anaconda Standard, February 11, 1900. The Anaconda Standard newspaper can be relied upon to be the most accurate and comprehensive account of Johnston's experience. It reflects an excellent global rendition of the entire event and includes many subtleties hitherto unmentioned in other "accounts" detailing how Johnston earned the name "Liver-Eating."

80. "How Liver-Eating Johnson Got His Name." November 30, 1939, Billings Times.

81. Virginia City Madisonian News, February 8, 1900. (article only - no page indicated).

82. Dillon Examiner, Dillon, Montana, 1915

83. The Post, December 25, 1884, Billings, Montana, Vol. III, No. 45, p. 1.

84. "The Scout's Life: General Sturgis Talks About the late 'Liver-Eating' Johnston,' January 25, 1878, The Daily Leader (article only – no page indicated)

85. Roy P. Johnson, North Dakota History, Vol. 16, No.2, April 1949, (State Historical Society of North Dakota, Bismark, ND), p. 96.

86. With the Indian Wars effectively over in October 1877 with the surrender of Chief Joseph, Johnston continued to hunt and trap. During trapping "off-season," Johnston served as guide either to the US Government or to private parties seeking adventure. Vic Smith, 1997, p. 86.

87. Glendolin D. Wagner and William A. Allen, 1933. Blankets and Moccasins: Plenty Coups and His People, The Crows. (Lincoln, Univ. of Neb). p. 167.

88. Helen F. Sanders, 1913, p. 141.

89. Glendolin D. Wagner and William A. Allen, 1933, pgs. 176-177.

CHAPTER 7

90. Johnston's reputation and frontier acumen allowed him to traverse the wilderness with reckless confidence. Because he was deemed "bad medicine" by his Indian foe, Johnston roamed wherever he pleased. and, when attacked, always claimed victory. J.W. Reddington. 1923, Way Out West - Remembrances and Tales, (New York, The Lewis Publishing Co.), p. 37.
91. The Lethbridge Daily Herald, Saturday, May 14, 1910.
92. R.M. Husbandman, Benton Crowd Jobbed Butter-In Using Liver-Eating Johnson as Stooge to End Competition, March 3, 1938 (no page indicated).

CHAPTER 8

93. Vic Smith, p. 67
94. Edward S. Bernard, Ed., 1977, Story of the Great American West (Pleasantville, Readers Digest), p. 236.
95. Vic Smith, p. 67.
96. Jerome Greene, 1991, p. 157.
97. Luther S. Kelly, 1926, p. 160.
98. Jerome Greene, 1991, pgs. 155-156.
99. Ibid. 1991, p. 165
100. Charles Erskine Scott Wood, "Appendix" in Chester Anders Lee, Chief Joseph: The Biography of a Great Indian, (New York: Wilson Erickson), 1936.
101. Jerome Greene, p. 228
102. Vic Smith, 1997, pgs. 78-79
103. Liver-Eating Johnston was recruited as a guide for General Howard upon joining the "Yellowstone Scouts." Scouts generally signed agreements to work in one-month periods. Because Johnston was a "contract" scout, i.e., independent of the Army, he was free to come and go as he pleased. Service as a guide usually did not include involvement in battles. Merril D. Beal, 1963, *I Will Fight No More Forever: Chief Joseph and the Nez Perce War,* (Seattle, University of Washington Press, p. 191.)

104. Mark H. Brown, *The Flight of the Nez Perce*, 1982, University of Nebraska Press, (Lincoln, Nebraska), p. 341

105. Yellowstone Genealogy, Roots Web, *Joseph M.V. Cochran – First Homesteader.*

106. Hugh Scott, 1928, " *Some Memories of a Soldier, "* (New York, The Century Co.), pgs. 80-81.

CHAPTER 9

107. Billings Gazette, November 10, 1940 (article only -no page number).

108. Myrtle E. Cooper, 1981, From Tent Town to City: A Chronological History of Billings, Montana, -1882- 1935 (Billings, Self- Published) p. 7.

109. Ibid. 1981, p. l.

110. Carrol Van West, 1993, Capitalism on the Frontier: Billings & the Yellowstone Valley in the Nineteenth Century (Lincoln, University of Nebraska Press), p. 54.

111. Johnston most likely arrived in Coulson soon after Muggins Taylor died on October 1, 1882. Myrtle E. Cooper, 1981, p. 8.

112. Ben Greenough, April 1951, "Liver-Eating Johnson," Pony Express, San Francisco, CA.,

113. Charles Spenser Tates, 1905, Pickway: A True Narrative, (Golden Rule Press), pgs. 25-28.

114. "Liver-Eating Johnson: The Career of a Yellowstone County Man As Pictured in a Leading Eastern Journal." February 24, 1900, Billings Weekly Gazette.

115. Harry Owens, 1983, *"The Saga of Liver Eating Johnston: He Never Ate Crow, "* Old West, Vol. 19, p. 16.

116. Ibid., p. 16 117. Carbon County Democrat, February 7, 1900. p. 11.

118. "As It Was In Billings 45 Years Ago," Billings Gazette, June 16, 1927.

119. Joyce M. Jensen, 1994, pgs. 38-39.

120. E.A. Brinstool, Fighting Indian Warriors, Indian Head Books, New York, NY. 1953, pgs. 289-290.

121. Harry Owens, p. 16

122. Billings Gazette, November 10, 1940.

123. Joyce M. Jensen, 1994, p. 40.

124. Billings Gazette, October 13, 1885

125. Vic Smith, p. 145

126. Myrtle E. Cooper, 1981, p. 24.

127. Declaration for the Increase of an Invalid Pension, April 10, 1889, Certificate No. 292234. Monthly Pension = $6.00 per month.

128. Declaration for Invalid Pension, April 9, 1890, Certificate No. 292234. Monthly Pension = $8.00 per month.

129. Declaration for Increase of Pension (Old and New Disabilities), July 29, 1895, Certificate No. 292234. Monthly Pension = $12.00

130. Rex Bundy, March 1977, p. 11.

131. Harry Owens, 1983, p. 16.

132. Ben Greenough, 1961, Pony Express

133. Ann Fendrich, The Cody Rustler, Monday, January 30, 1967, p. 1

134. Red Lodge: Tales of the First 100 Years," 1988, Carbon County News, Vol. xxix.

135. Tombstone Prospector, November 1, 1895, p. 4, Col.1

CHAPTER 10

136. Marvin Pelo, August 1990. "Liver-Eatin' Saved a Family," Montana Free Press (article only -no page indicated).

137. Declaration For the Increase of and Invalid Pension, November 15, 1899. Monthly Pension = $12.00

138. "Liver-Eating Johnson: A Tribute from Col. Sam Gates of Miles City," November 29, 1899, Carbon County Democrat, p.7.

139. "Liver-Eating Johnson: The Old Scout Starts for the California Soldiers' Home," December 13, 1899, Carbon County Democrat Vol. I, P. 1.

140. Bynum Herald, March 27, 1922.

CHAPTER 11

141. Don Haley, 7 March 1974, "Students Hope To Move Body of Liver-Eating (Jeremiah) Johnson." Antelope Valley Press, Section 1, p. 10.

142. R.C. House, October 1990, "Pioneer Reburied in Land He Loved," *The National Tombstone Epitaph, pgs.* 15- 16.

143. Don Haley, 7 March 1974, *Antelope Valley Press, Section* I, p. 10.

CHAPTER 12

144. Jack Anderson, 19 June 1974, "Indian Fighter's Reburial Illegal," Rocky Mountain News

145. Sylvia Beeler, 3 April 1975, "County Profile: Jeremiah Johnson – John Johnston – 1824-1900," Snake River Press, p. 3.

146. Enterprise, June 12, 1974 (no author or page indicated).

147. Gary Svee, 9 June 1974, "Johnson Lives On," Billings Gazette.

148. Carbon County News, June 13, 1974.